T0137656

Life-Style Evangelism

Life-Style Evangelism

Crossing Traditional Boundaries

to Reach the Unbelieving World

Joseph C. Aldrich

MULTNOMAH
BOOKS

LIFESTYLE EVANGELISM

© 1981, 1993

Published by Multnomah Books

International Standard Book Number: 978-1-59052-754-2

Published in the United States by WaterBrook Multnomah,
an imprint of the Crown Publishing Group, a division
of Random House LLC, New York,
a Penguin Random House Company.

MULTNOMAH and its mountain colophon are registered
trademarks of Random House LLC.

Multnomah Books
12265 Oracle Boulevard, Suite 200
Colorado Springs, CO 80921

146086900

To Roland Niednagel,
a dear brother and fellow evangelist
whose continued encouragement
prompted the writing of this book

Contents

Read This First

Evangelistic effectiveness eludes all too many of us in the body of Christ. Because we have a nagging suspicion that we should do better, we devise a number of reasons to explain away our failure to witness. We may even have our favorite collection of Bible verses which prove: 1) the world will always be hostile to the gospel, 2) not many enter the Kingdom, 3) the command to evangelize is restricted in its application, and most importantly, 4) we probably don't have the gift.

Joe Aldrich challenges those dearly held beliefs with scriptures that exhort us to follow Jesus Christ and his disciples—next door, across the street, into the rest of the world—and take his love and message of hope as our calling cards. When we do, the lives of those we contact will never be the same. Take Lou, for example, founder and vice-chairman of a Fortune 500 company:

> *Joe Aldrich has been the most meaningful person in my life. I became a born-again Christian by accepting Jesus Christ as my personal Savior in Joe's office after his suggestion that I should trust Christ. Ever since Joe has taken me—maybe the worst of all sinners—and loved me into a personal relationship with Jesus Christ, I have lived an entirely new and abundant life (John 10:10).*
>
> *Before becoming a Christian, I thought I had everything: family, good health, three houses, six boats, four cars, and a successful business. But even with all of these good things, something was missing inside. Now I know the real meaning of life, and that is life in Christ. I would gladly trade all my materialistic things for the relationship with God I now have. Joe was there to share and listen when I needed him.*

Families have also been affected by Joe and his wife Ruthe. This testimony from Linda is a good example of the kind of life-changing influence God can bring when the principles of *Life-Style Evangelism* are put into action:

Several years ago I moved into a lovely apartment with a load of dreams. My dental student husband was in his senior year and we had decided to treat ourselves to luxuries—a swimming pool and a dishwasher—for the last few months before his graduation. I dreamed of soon quitting my secretarial job and starting a family. But all my dreams exploded just a few weeks later when my husband moved out and filed for a divorce. When the rent was due that month, I revealed my tragedy to the managers of the apartment, a seminary student and a school teacher, named Joe and Ruthe Aldrich.

Ruthe empathized with the heartache and loneliness I felt; she genuinely cared. She told me that she believed her own marriage worked because she and Joe put Christ at the center of it. I didn't understand, but it sounded good.

Ruthe stopped by often to check on me, and she and Joe began to take me out to dinner and have me over for meals. As they opened their lives to me, I knew I had found some special friends, unlike any I'd ever known. They always cared and had time to listen to me and even cry with me. From the close vantage point they gave me of their lives, I knew there was something about them and their marriage that I truly wanted. The books and Bible verses they gave me were wrapped in their constant love. Eventually I asked them about their relationship to Christ. It was so simple and clear when they came to Revelation 3:20 that I had no doubt what my response was to be. That night I invited Christ into my life.

Though I had hoped my problems would be over the next day, they weren't. My marriage never mended and I struggled over my future. But I knew I was a new creature and had been given a fresh start by Christ. The support and encouragement of Ruthe and Joe kept me going. I began to see God's Spirit at work in my life and I wanted to share what I'd found. I wanted to learn to love and care for others—just like the Aldriches had loved and cared for me.

That spring and summer, the three of us spent time getting better acquainted with our neighbors. People opened up to us with questions about our faith when we took the time to invite them over for hamburgers. Several made quiet commitments to Christ during the course of the Bible study Joe taught at my apartment.

I am now married to a wonderful Christian man and have a six-year-old son. Our thirteen-year marriage has not been problem-free, but God has helped us work through the difficulties as I've practiced Joe and Ruthe's plan—putting Christ at the center of our marriage. As we have learned to communicate this reality of our faith to others, God continues to bring us back to the same costly kind of evangelism Ruthe and Joe used to minister to me: mixing the Good News with love, care, and friendship.

Joe's biblical philosophy of evangelism has helped not only businessmen and families, it has also helped pastors. Gary, a pastor in Corvallis, Oregon, tells how:

My wife and I attended a conference for pastors in Colorado where Joe Aldrich was the speaker. There we accepted the challenge to begin praying for at least five couples in our neighborhood. We had previously made contact with a number of them, but had not prayed much for them. We had not been ready "to give an answer for the hope that is within us."

Since that conference, God has given us some amazing opportunities. One of the most exciting is a developing relationship with a family from Chile. My wife has been meeting with the wife from this family each Wednesday afternoon, helping her to learn English by reading the Bible. She and her husband are deeply appreciative, and they have begun to ask a number of questions about spiritual things.

I have challenged the students in my high school class to write on a bookmark in their Bible the names of people for whom they will pray and be available neighbors. Three weeks ago a brother of one girl in the class and the woman he was living with both made a commitment to Christ. They have now begun attending our church. We're excited at what God is doing!

Joe Aldrich would disclaim any credit for the above stories, other than that he does believe in being available to be used by God in people's lives. This is the pattern set before us by Jesus Christ in his earthly life.

If you are concerned about evangelism, if you are concerned about people, if you are concerned about God's plan for men on earth, give this book a fair reading. You may change your views. Then, quite possibly, God can use you in the lives of nonbelievers—so they will believe.

The Publisher

Foreword

If Jesus appeared on earth today as he did two thousand years ago, many churches would not elect him to their official boards. He would have disqualified himself because he ran with the wrong crowd.

The historian Luke comments that tax collectors and sinners—folks shunned by religious types because they had made a mess of life—kept seeking him out to hear what he had to say. When they came to him, Jesus gave them a hearty welcome and often enjoyed dinner with them. Socializing with people like that ruined his testimony. The Pharisees and Bible teachers who observed him wrote off his association with that element of society as a secret sympathy with sin. Yet, the fact remains Jesus went out of his way to cultivate those relationships, and if we are serious about following him, we must do the same.

Making a place in your life for non-Christian neighbors demands effort, thought, and at times risk. Bridges are harder to construct than walls. But that doesn't alter this reality: Outsiders to faith are first drawn to Christians and then to Christ. Unfortunately, not all Christians attract. Like a turned magnet, some repel. Yet Christians, alive to God, loving, caring, laughing, sharing, involved at the point of people's needs, present an undeniable witness for Christ in their society.

Developing a life style to make that happen is what this book is all about. That is why thoughtful Christians will read it, and that is why neighbors who live next door or share a ride with us or work with us may thank God we did.

Dr. Haddon W. Robinson
Gordon-Conwell Theological Seminary

The Enterprise Called Evangelism

*T*here is a legend which recounts the return of Jesus to glory after his time on earth. Even in heaven he bore the marks of his earthly pilgrimage with its cruel cross and shameful death. The angel Gabriel approached him and said, "Master, you must have suffered terribly for men down there."

"I did," he said.

"And," continued Gabriel, "do they know all about how you loved them and what you did for them?"

"Oh, no," said Jesus, "not yet. Right now only a handful of people in Palestine know."

Gabriel was perplexed. "Then what have you done to let everyone know about your love for them?"

Jesus said, "I've asked Peter, James, John, and a few more friends to tell other people about me. Those who are told will in turn tell still other people, and my story will be spread to the farthest reaches of the globe. Ultimately, all of mankind will have heard about my life and what I have done."

Gabriel frowned and looked rather skeptical. He knew well what poor stuff men were made of. "Yes," he said, "but what if Peter and James and John grow weary? What if the people who come after them forget? Haven't you made any other plans?"

Jesus answered, "I have no other plans. I'm counting on them." Twenty centuries later, he still has no other plan. He's counting on you and me. High on God's "To Do" list is the evangelization of the world. His early disciples adopted his priorities and devoted themselves to reaching their world. Christ counted on them, and they delivered. Have we done as well?

Too Many People

Before we succumb to another guilt trip, let's consider some reasons why we appear ineffective when compared to the apostles. Our purpose is not to excuse ourselves but to understand some of the forces or influences which hinder our effectiveness.

First, the need to relate to the ever-increasing number of people in our daily experience has crippled our ability to relate effectively to even one person. Excessive relational demands have crippled our relational capacities. There are simply too many people. A casual stroll down the street brings me face to face with dozens of people every minute. I cannot possibly recognize or relate to them. I must pass by them and treat them as indifferently as parts of machinery moving down an assembly line. To make matters worse, population densities of most metropolitan areas reinforce alienation and indifference.

This attitude of isolation becomes a way of life. I don't want to bother you, and I don't want you to bother me. Am I my brother's keeper? By all means—no! Unable to relate to the hordes of people, my mind concludes that there are no people. Asia's teeming millions don't exist. "What people? I don't see any people." One million people become zero.

This response of unconcern may be necessary to maintain some sort of psychological equilibrium, but it hurts the evangelistic enterprise. Relationships are critical to the gospel's impact, yet most Christians have neither significant contacts with non-Christians nor the ability to relate in a redemptive manner.

Stop the World—I Can't Get Off

A second reason for ineffectiveness is the pace of life: It is too fast and complicated. Technological acceleration has directly affected our way of living. Jobs change, people move, congestion grows, traffic jams. Telephones ring incessantly, and the TV drones on and on whether watched or not. Held captive by schedules and the demands of others, we find ourselves unable to slow our world and get off. Add to this swift pace the complexities of our world's problems. News reports of crises around the world and next door jam our mental capacities beyond their load limit. We are inundated with problems beyond our comprehension and sense that no one has the solution.

Caught up in a whirlwind of activity, schedules, and events, we find that healthy, supportive, "people" time is an increasingly rare commodity. Adding evangelism to an already hectic schedule would be the straw that breaks the camel's back.

Aquariums, Ambushes, and Safaris

A third source of ineffectiveness in evangelism is our exposure to unhealthy evangelism models. The evangelism options as presented and practiced only provide realistic opportunities for a small percentage of the Christian community. Although many of the evangelism practices "work," in some cases they actually hinder the total impact of a given church in a community. While some churches fail to grow because they do not evangelize, others fail to grow because they do—but in outmoded, ineffective forms.

For many, evangelism is what the pastor does on Sunday morning as he throws the lure over the pulpit, hoping some fish in the stained-glass aquarium will bite. The layman's job is simply to herd fish within the reach of the big fisherman. Week after week the pastor evangelizes the evangelized. His people will grow weak on a diet of evangelistic sermons, unable to witness effectively about the reality of the full-orbed gospel in their own lives. The starved church members "are unable to witness to the good news…[because] they are not experiencing it."[1] It is a strange phenomenon indeed for a church group whose major emphasis is evangelism.

The truth is that everything that happens, teaches. If the only means of evangelism is the big fisherman in the pulpit, he may catch some; but he is teaching by his actions an approach to evangelism which may hinder the evangelistic potential of his local fellowship. Evangelism is contextual, and without careful attention to the beauty of the body (edification), evangelistic efforts become increasingly contrived, unnatural, and ineffective. Effective individual evangelism grows out of the context of a healthy, vibrant fellowship of believers. The impact of a church's evangelistic efforts is directly proportional to the health of its corporate life.

Another potentially unhealthy evangelism model is what I call the ambush method. The non-Christian is invited to an event where a high-powered speaker unloads both barrels. Often the guest has no idea of the purpose of the invitation and feels trapped and embarrassed. This method reminds some of sawdust trails or scalding tears fueled by people skilled in manipulation of both emotions and Scripture.

Many assume that evangelism is what Billy Graham does and thus remove themselves from involvement because they don't have his gifts. Sometimes the only exposure to evangelism for believers is being part of a weekly task force on a spiritual safari into enemy territory. On such forays total strangers are confronted with a verbal message said to be the gospel. Some such experiences of evangelism are valid, and God blesses. Many are not, though, and represent an unbalanced, unnatural, and in some cases, unbiblical approach to reaching people.

Many believers have been burned by an unfortunate experience of attempting to evangelize someone, and they have given up. Often this bad experience is the result of a failure to distinguish between witnessing and soul winning. "As long as a man simply tells another about Jesus, he is a witness. But the moment he tries to get that person to do something with Christ, he shifts over to the role of the soul winner."[2] Witnessing and soul winning are two different specialties. Many have been taught that evangelism equals soul winning and have tried soul winning with disastrous results. Embarrassed and humiliated, they have withdrawn completely from anything to do with evangelism.

Unhealthy evangelism models have hurt the evangelism enterprise. Often the artificial and unnatural methodology of some of these models offends the sensitivities of caring Christians. Gimmicks, pseudo-questionnaires, buttonholing, evangelical mugging, and the outright rudeness of some witnesses turn them off. The result is that evangelism becomes a much misunderstood term—one most people either swear by… or at.

Separation or Segregation

Perceived cultural barriers and outright theological errors combine to make the fourth ineffective factor which short-circuits evangelism. The majority of Christians have lost their ability to relate significantly to non-Christians. By no stretch of the imagination can the Christian community be called the "salt of the earth."

For salt to be effective, it must get out of its container and into the world of hurting, dying, suffering, sinning people. There is no impact without contact, and yet, after knowing the Lord two years, the average Christian has no significant relationships with non-Christians. Often conversion opens up a whole new web of relationships and the new Christian inadvertently drifts away from his non-Christian associates. In some cases the nature of his past associations makes separation a necessity if growth is to take place. All too often, however, he withdraws from significant contact because his local church misunderstands the biblical doctrine of separation.

Frequently the unsaved are viewed as enemies rather than victims of the Enemy. Spirituality is viewed as separation from the unsaved. The new Christian is told he has nothing in common with his unsaved associates. Frankly, I have a lot in common with them: a mortgage, car payments, kids who misbehave, a lawn to mow, a car to wash, a less-than-perfect marriage, a few too many pounds around my waist, and an interest in sports, hobbies, and other activities they enjoy. It is well to remember that Jesus was called a "friend of sinners." A friend of sinners. Selah!

Bridging the Credibility Gap

A fifth cause of a weakened evangelistic enterprise is the imbalance between the verbalization and the incarnation of the gospel. Christians are to be good news before they share the good news. The words of the gospel are to be incarnated before they are verbalized. The music of the gospel must precede the words of the gospel and prepare the context in which there will be a hunger for those words.

What is the music of the gospel? The music of the gospel is the beauty of the indwelling Christ as lived out in the everyday relationships of life. The gospel is the good news that Jesus Christ has solved the problem of man's sin and offers him the potential of an exchanged life, a life in which the resources of God himself are available for his transformation. And as the gospel is translated into music, it makes redemptive relationships possible. When the world observes husbands loving their wives, and wives supporting and caring for their husbands and families, they have seen a miracle; they have heard the music. It is miraculous music for which many of them are longing.

The two greatest forces in evangelism are a healthy church and a healthy marriage. The two are interdependent. You can't have one without the other. The healthy marriage, however, is the front-lines weapon. The Christian family in a community is the ultimate evangelistic tool, assuming the home circle is an open one in which the beauty of the gospel is readily available. It's the old story: When love is seen, the message is heard.

Even God's evangelism strategy in the Old and New Testament involves a beautiful bride and her relationship to him. Israel and the church are called "brides" by God and their beauty is of great concern to him. But the beauty described (Ezekiel 16, Ephesians 5) is relational. It is the beauty of how they lived together. Israel became a harlot because she forgot the source of her beauty and splendor. The church at Ephesus was charged with the loss of beauty even though she was theologically sound (the condition of hundreds of churches today).

Most evangelism training involves helping people learn how to say the words of the gospel. Little attention is paid to developing a biblical philosophy of ministry which moves the corporate life of the church away from ugliness to beauty. We must become candidates for God's blessing, begin to incarnate his beauty in our relationships, and open these relationships to the non-Christian.

Once the music has been heard, expect to be asked for the "reason for the hope (beauty) that you have."

Play the music, and they'll be candidates for the Word! Sheldon Vanauken says it so well: "The best argument for Christianity is Christians; their joy, their certainty, their completeness. But the strongest argument against Christianity is also Christians—when they are sombre and joyless, when they are self-righteous and smug in complacent consecration, when they are narrow and repressive, then Christianity dies a thousand deaths."[3]

When the joy, the certainty, the completeness, and the beauty of a Christian community is cultivated and communicated, evangelism is the glorious result. I have written this book to nudge the church toward its divine birthright so that it will explode its beauty into Jerusalem, Judea, Samaria, and the uttermost parts of your world.

Notes

1. James Engel, *Contemporary Christian Communications* (Nashville: Thomas Nelson, Inc., 1979), 27.

2. C. S. Lovett, *Witnessing Made Easy* (Baldwin Park, Calif.: Personal Christianity, 1979), 20.

3. Sheldon Vanauken, *A Severe Mercy* (New York: Harper and Row, 1977), 85.

Part 1

Evangelism as It Should Be

Embarking on a Pilgrimage to Beauty

What do Cinderella, princesses kissing frogs, and ugly ducklings have in common? All three describe a pilgrimage to beauty. Why does the delightful story of Cinderella endear itself to the hearts of millions of people around the world? Because one persistent prince is able to transform a lowly, unkempt, awkward servant girl into a charming, beautiful, graceful princess. Whether it be princesses kissing frogs, ugly ducklings becoming swans, or abused Cinderellas becoming belles of the ball, beauty is always irresistible. Its secrets are priceless, its presence is magnetic. It should come as no surprise, then, that God's strategy for evangelism involves a beautiful bride.

A beautiful bride—that's the key to evangelism. Brides bypass intellects and capture hearts. Tough, calloused, hardened men are known to weep in their presence. Men of steel melt and their wives get misty-eyed. Ideally, a bride is the epitome of all that is right and beautiful. She's a symbol of purity, hope, purpose, trust, love, beauty, and wholeness in a world pockmarked with ugliness. The bride motif, found in both testaments, is used by God to illustrate his strategy for attracting mankind to his life-changing grace.

The name of God's bride in the Old Testament is Israel. In the New Testament it is the church. Both Israel and the church are described as brides whose beauty is traced to God's love for them. Our focus for the moment is the church. Paul tells us that Christ loved the church and gave himself for her to "present her to himself as a radiant church, without stain or wrinkle or any other blemish, but holy and blameless" (Ephesians 5:27). This verse about Christ's love for the church has great bearing upon God's evangelism strategy.

THE CALLING FORTH OF BEAUTY

Carefully take note of the purpose, the product, and the process of Christ's love. The *purpose* of Christ's love is to call forth beauty (without stain or wrinkle). The *product* of Christ's love is said to be "holiness and blamelessness." "Holy" describes the *character* of the church; "blameless" describes her *conduct*. Christ's love of his bride is the *process* by which he develops her holy character and blameless conduct.

As a successful agent for change, there is nothing comparable to love. Its transforming power is beautifully real—and miraculously effective. Years ago a stray dog adopted the nine Aldrich children. Obviously mistreated and suffering from malnutrition, the dog's reactions made it clear love was not part of its daily experience. With its tail between its legs, it would slink around, cowering as though it expected to be struck, abused, or driven away. We named the dog Tex and started loving our newest family member as only kids can do. We weren't psychologists, nor did we know of love's power to change. We just liked animals. But love won out and Tex was transformed into a different dog. Eager to join our every antic, quick to trust our leadership in each situation, and overflowing with love that came in the form of licks and enthusiastic nuzzles, Tex literally became a new creature when love became a part of his experience. We too can be transformed by this process. Broken by sin and blemished by infinite imperfections, we have not been excluded from Christ's love.

Love involves nourishing and cherishing. The word *nourish* describes the *actions* of his love. To nourish means to provide all that is necessary for growth. Love involves action, and loving actions encourage and produce growth. *Cherish* describes Christ's *attitude* toward the objects of his love. Isn't it incredible to think that he cherished us? That he goes the extra mile for us? That he considers us of great value and worth to him? As objects of his love we grow and become beautiful—that is, holy and blameless.

WHAT IS HOLINESS?

Holiness is primarily a statement about the moral condition of a person. But it does have visible, observable dimensions. One synonym for holiness is *wholeness.* We all appreciate wholesome, balanced people. The term portrays one who is functioning according to divine intention, one who is fulfilling his intended purpose. A man who is holy will be growing in his ability to act and function as a whole, integrated, balanced person. Such growth is an observable miracle because no man can reverse the progressive disintegration, separation, and isolation sin produces. Genuine holiness is not static. Translated into life and action, it manifests itself through such qualities as integrity, justice, right-eousness, and freedom from guilt. In summary, a truly holy person is a *wholesome* person.

Holiness is the basis or foundation of blamelessness. One cannot be both blameless and unholy. When we say a person is blameless, we usually mean that his behavior is beyond repute. No one can point an accusing finger at him. His holy character (his basic essence) expresses itself through his blameless conduct. It is also a relational term in that it *presupposes* interaction and rela-tionship with people, events, and circumstances. An elder is required to have the quality of "blamelessness" (Titus 1:7). The term suggests the possibility (and the necessity) of living life to the fullest, and yet not compromising the boundary conditions of God's character. Positionally, the believer stands blameless before God because of Christ's substitutionary death. Practically, blame-lessness is a verdict reached by those who observe a life and compare it to a standard. Such a person or group has credibility, the first essential for effective evangelism. We must *be* good news before we share it.

When an individual, a family, or a body of believers are moving together toward wholeness (holiness), a credible life style emerges (blamelessness), and their potential for effective witness (beauty) increases dramatically. Because this is true, *evangelism is a way of living beautifully and opening one's web of relationships to include the nonbeliever. A person is exposed to both the music and the words of the gospel.* God begins the process and we become the whole and wholesome product. All for the purpose of displaying his beauty.

GOD'S CATALYST OF LOVE

God's love is the catalyst which makes a pilgrimage toward holiness and blamelessness a human possibility. The theme of Israel as God's bride is useful here. The prophet Ezekiel graphically describes God's efforts to make Israel beautiful (Ezekiel 16). He reminds Israel that God rescued her from the rubbish heap where she had been abandoned and left to die. The rescued infant grew under God's nurture and care and came to be "old enough for love." God entered into a covenant with her, and she became his bride. God lavishly poured out his wealth and resources upon her, the object of his love, and she "became very beautiful and rose to be a queen" (Ezekiel 16:13). From the rubbish heap to royalty! The familiar words "Do I love you because you are beautiful, or are you beautiful because I love you?" are freighted with significance. Yes, we become beautiful as God loves us.

What an incredible journey. It's the good news journey offered to every man and woman, every boy and girl. It's the gospel in a nutshell. God is in the business of transforming rubbish-heap rejects into royalty through the mystery of the new birth.

With royalty came *recognition*. God put Israel on display. "And your fame spread among the nations on account of your beauty, because the splendor I had given you made your beauty perfect" (Ezekiel 16:14). What did the world see when Israel's beauty was on display? The splendor of God himself. How was it seen? It was displayed through Israel's culture and institutions. Her courts of law revealed the justice and holiness of God. Her artistic expressions (the glorious tabernacle and temple, for example) revealed the order, symmetry, and beauty of God. Israel's sociological patterns of marriage and family, her care for the infants and the aged pointed to her God. Israel's relationships to other nations pointed to the covenant-keeping nature of God (as well as his hatred of unrighteousness). Israel's law with its exalted views of personal value and dignity was part of God's reflected beauty. Israel's code of business ethics as recorded in her laws was another facet of God's splendor at work in human affairs.

In a nutshell, Israel's beauty was the beauty of a redeemed people living, acting, and relating in concert with divine will. To be effective in evangelism, we must practice the art of influencing the unsaved in accord with the aesthetic sense with which God has endowed his creatures. They respond to beauty!

Look at that remarkable statement again: "The splendor I had given you made your beauty perfect." *Beauty is the possession and expression of the nature of God.* Faith in Christ makes me a partaker of God's nature. God himself comes to indwell me and manifest his life and love through me. Through the new birth, I have a great treasure (indwelling Holy Spirit) in an earthen vessel (me). I'm a clay pot indwelt by the Almighty God who loves me!

Evangelism is *expressing* what I possess in Christ and *explaining* how I came to possess it. In the truest sense, evangelism is displaying the universals of God's character—his love, his righteousness, his justice, and his faithfulness—through the particulars of my everyday life. Therefore evangelism is not a special activity to be undertaken at a prescribed time. It is the constant and spontaneous outflow of our individual and corporate experience of Christ. Even more specifically, evangelism is what Christ does *through* the activity of his children as they are involved in 1) proclamation, 2) fellowship, and 3) service.

SPREADING THE BEAUTY AROUND

God does not intend for his message of beauty to stagnate. After catalyzing with his love the process of beauty in an individual and a group, he casts forth his people as seed—seed that will grow into a beautiful message. The first two parables of Matthew 13 teach us that God sows two kinds of seed: *a blessed message* and *a beautiful man.* In the first parable the seed sown is primarily a verbal message, the gospel of the kingdom. The focus of this parable is upon the receptivity of the soil (the target audience) and the factors which influence receptivity. Forces are described which thwart the evangelistic enterprise. Satan works to remove truth. The pressures and afflictions of life and materialistic priorities resist the potential fruitfulness of the gospel. All of us have experienced these struggles in our personal pilgrimages.

But some do respond to the message, and through faith in Christ come to *possess* the nature of God. As they grow (as edification takes place), they begin to *express* what they possess. The nature of God becomes operational and observable in the practical, everyday events of their lives. What a joy it is to see a new creature in Christ begin to change, to grow, to move toward wholeness. As the Spirit schedules surgery, masks come off, bad habits begin to disappear, attitudes change, and relationships begin to improve. These who respond to the seed (verbal message) of the first parable *become* the seed (the message) in the second parable.

The "good seed" of the second parable are called "the sons of the kingdom" (Matthew 13:38). Jesus Christ is the one who sows the good seed and his field is the world (note that Satan follows the same strategy). The qualifying adjective "good" indicates that God's strategy is not simply to sow in a specific geographical area a mouth that moves on cue. The word translated "good" is one of the Greeks' favorite terms for beauty. Beautiful seeds *are produced* as they respond to the gospel and *become productive* as they are sown by Christ to reveal his beauty as he did his Father's.

You are God's seed, friend. God wants to take a radical idea (his plan of redemption), clothe it with flesh and blood, and turn it loose in the world of men. What a privilege—and what an opportunity! *You* have been put on display, cast as good seed into this world's field, and set as a shining lamp in a world of blackness.

CHRIST'S PERSONAL PROGRAM OF BEAUTIFICATION

God's Son blazed a trail for us during his pilgrimage through this earth's perpetual darkness. He was the Word, God's message in human flesh. His actions were observed and his words were heard. The call of God upon us is a call to share his mission in the world. "First, He sent His Son. Then He sent His Spirit. Now He sends His church, that is, us. He sends us out by His Spirit into His world to announce His Son's salvation—He worked through His Son to achieve it; He works through us to make it known." [1] Besides bringing redemption, Christ came to make visible, to reveal, and to communicate the heart, the essence, the being of the invisible God. His strategy is instructive for us because his mission was the prototype of ours: "As you sent me into the world, I have sent them into the world" (John 17:18; cf. 20:21).

Christ's model helps us see that effective evangelism involves the *visualization* and *verbalization* of truth. Christ's personal communication strategy was incarnational: "The Word became flesh and made his dwelling among us. We have seen his glory, the glory of the One and Only, who came from the Father, full of grace and truth" (John 1:14). In this verse, we have a model for evangelism. It declares Christ's *purpose:* to glorify his Father. It sets forth his *strategy:* to incarnate the truth (to become flesh). And it describes his *methodology:* to be full of grace and truth.

The Word became flesh. Jesus Christ became the visible expression of the invisible God. This was his strategy. He told his disciples, "Anyone who has seen me has seen the Father" (John 14:9). He was, as it were, a visual aid to reveal the nature of his Father. He didn't just talk about love; he loved. And the sinners considered him their friend. He didn't just preach on forgiveness; he forgave. And sinful, guilt-ridden people fell at his feet, forgiven and cleansed. He didn't just proclaim the necessity of justice and righteousness; he attacked the unrighteous institutions of his day. He didn't start a Bible institute and establish a chair of theology in his Father's name; he invited men to live with him twenty-four hours a day. His strategy was to become flesh and live among them.

The term "live among" could be translated, "to pitch a tent." It is used in the Greek translation of the Old Testament to describe the tabernacle where God's presence "lived among" them. The tabernacle was the shrine of God's glory. Like the Old Testament tabernacle, Jesus became the shrine of his Father's glory. (Is there any "glory beheld" if there is no "pitching among"?)

How again did the Father send him? Essentially he became one of us. "The Word became flesh. God did not send a telegram or shower evangelistic Bible study books from heaven or drop a million bumper stickers from the sky saying, 'Smile, Jesus loves you.' He sent a man, His Son, to communicate the message. His strategy has not changed. He still sends men and women—before he sends tracts and techniques—to change the world. You may think His strategy is risky—but that is God's problem, not yours."[2]

In John 9:5, Christ declares that while he is in the world, he is the light of the world. The evening before his death, he told his disciples, "You are going to have the light just a little while longer" (John 12:35). With his ascension, the "light of the world" left. But his purposes march on! Ephesians 5:8 says, "but now you are light in the Lord. Live as children of light." As children of light (1 Thessalonians 5:5), we are not to hide our lights (the beauty of what we possess) under a bushel. Christ now plants his good seed as lights so that they can "bring salvation to the ends of the earth" (Acts 13:47). In a very real sense, Christ has no feet but our feet, he has no tongue but our tongue.

Full of grace and truth. John helps us understand *what* people observed (the glory) by saying that Jesus was full of *grace* and *truth.* It does not say he was "full of facts and figures," although he was. Certainly Christ as "truth" has great theological significance. He is and embodies all truth. He is the supreme, ultimate revelation of his Father. Jesus teaches us by his life that not only is it important that we understand and proclaim truth, but that *we ourselves become truth.* It is always easier to study and comprehend the truth than it is to *be* truth.

The biblical terms for truth help us understand what it means to *be* truth. The Greek word for truth is *aletheia.* The basic meaning focuses on what is open to view, what is unconcealed and transparent. Certainly part of "being truth" is a commitment to avoid falsehood and deception. An Old Testament passage illustrates this part of being truth. In Psalm 15:1-2 David writes: "LORD, who may dwell in your sanctuary? Who may live on your holy hill?" The answer is instructive. "He whose walk is blameless and who does what is righteous, who speaks the truth from his heart." Being truth involves at least three things: 1) walking blamelessly, 2) doing what is right, and 3) speaking truth from the heart.

Biblical Hebrew adds another facet to our understanding of what it means to *be* truth. The Hebrew word for truth is *emeth.* The root verb means to be secure, solid, or firm. The basic meaning is consistency or reliability. Our Lord is "full of truth." As such he is transparent—free of all deception with no intent to cover up or mislead. Likewise, he is totally reliable and can be counted upon to act consistently and blamelessly. The result of this proper blending of *grace* and *truth* is glory, the glory of the Father.

With the coming of Christ the Old Testament era ended. No longer was the sacrificial system necessary. The rent veil was God's declaration that the old dispensation was over. God's presence no longer is linked with inanimate, physical structures such as tabernacles or temples. God has moved. But not without leaving a forwarding address. You, dear one, are his home, the place where he has taken up residence.

What an incredible thought: My heart is Christ's home—Christ, full of grace and truth, lives here! We err when we call a church auditorium a "sanctuary." God no longer lives in sanctuaries made by men. He lives in you. You are the temple of God. As those who are indwelt by *The* Light of the world grow in grace and truth, they are "being transformed into his likeness with ever-increasing glory" (2 Corinthians 3:18).

Let's review for a moment. *Christ's purpose* was to declare his Father's glory. His *strategy* was to become flesh. His *methodology* was to be "full of grace and truth." He is by nature full of grace and truth. We are not. The effective evangelist must adopt Christ's purpose, accept his strategy, and develop his qualities. The following illustration depicts this program of beautification.

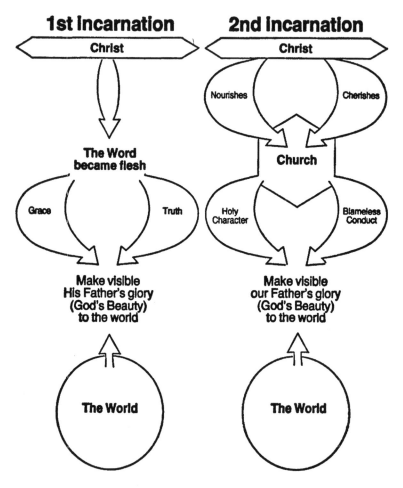

BECOMING BEFORE BROADCASTING

An illustration from the ancient Greek culture underscores the need for a communicator to embody his message. Even the pagan Greeks understood that the "medium is the message." Aristotle focused on three qualities of the successful communicator. First, he must have *ethos,* a term related to our word *ethical.* The finest communicator loses his credibility if his integrity is questionable.

The second quality of an effective communicator is *pathos*. This is the root from which we derive the terms *sympathy* and *empathy*. The listener wants to know if the speaker shares his hopes, yearnings, and longings. The Greeks recognized that oratorical skill without a caring heart added up to zero. Paul expressed the same thoughts when he wrote, "I am nothing" (1 Corinthians 13:1,2). Eloquence without love is worthless.

The effective member of the second incarnation must be an ethical, caring person. Floyd McClung said it well. "People don't care how much we know until they know how much we care." Do you care? Aristotle used pathos to refer to a response within the *listener.* I believe the quality of pathos is essential for the speaker as well. Aristotle believed that the listener, having been appealed to by the speaker's ethos and words, is persuaded when emotions within him are aroused in support of the speaker's message. The successful communicator both *has* and *appeals* to the quality called pathos.

Logia is the final quality of the effective communicator. Our term *logos* (word) comes from this word family. The one who communicates *must have something to say.* Ethos and pathos are character qualities and as such are observable. The non-Christian needs a demonstration, a visual aid which reveals that the gospel really is good news, that it really does address itself to the deepest needs and motives of the human heart. This new awareness is music to him, beautiful music! Such an exposure to truth incarnate helps prepare him to hear the words (the logia) of the gospel. It is my belief that if the beauty of the body is not taken seriously, the cause of world evangelism is ultimately futile.

Unfortunately, most evangelism courses focus on teaching the individual how to *say the words* of the gospel. Not many zero in on *how to play the music.* And the verbal *message* of the gospel without the *music* loses much of its impact. The Bible blends both together. For example, Peter says, "Always be prepared to give an answer [words] to everyone who asks you to give the reason for the hope [music] that you have" (1 Peter 3:15).

Peter also illustrates the power of the music when he encourages wives with spiritually indifferent husbands to shut off the words and play the music (1 Peter 3). The power of a redeemed, changed life is a strategic means of winning those who are spiritually indifferent. Peter underscores the magnetic power of beauty by encouraging women to develop inner beauty and use it as a positive force for change.

B E A U T Y   A S   A   W A Y   O F   L I F E

Another intriguing thought about a beautiful bride as the displayer of God's splendor is that *God's bride is not a person but people in relationship.* Consequently, the beauty described is one of corporate function and relationship rather than outward form and appearance. This is what our Lord meant when he said, "All men will know that you are my disciples if you meet on Sundays at 11:00 A.M. and 6:00 P.M." No, believe it or not, that is not what the text says. They will know . . . *if* you love one another.

Christ's bride is the church—people in relationship to one another. God has designed your relationships with other Christians as the primary context in which his nature surfaces and becomes tangible and observable. Not many nonbelievers are reading the revelation of God's graces revealed in Scripture. Many are reading the revelation of God revealed in your life and relationships. Like it or not, Scripture calls us *living epistles,* read (as a book) by all men. We are "Bible translators" for lost people. Evangelism, then, is stereophonic. God speaks to his creatures through two channels: the written Word, and you, his living epistle, his good seed. God's redemptive love is *declared* in Scripture, *demonstrated* at the Cross, and *displayed* in the body. God has chosen a bride. He desires to love forth its beauty. It is this beauty, the visualization of God's own beautiful and complete character, that communicates to an unheeding world. Christ has proven this method of evangelism; it remains for individuals and the church to embark upon the pilgrimage of beauty and thus become God's effective communicators of truth.

We will examine in later chapters the factors that contribute to a healthy evangelistic church and usher it along its journey toward beauty. But first we must clear the decks of the misconceptions that have marred the beautiful voyage for many. One

misconception is that believers must avoid life styles that penetrate the nonbelieving community. In addition, once we
acknowledge and understand that a penetrating life style is evangelistically effective, we must understand how it can be adopted.

Notes

1. John Stott, *Our Guilty Silence: The Church, the Gospel, and the World* (Grand Rapids: Wm. B. Eerdmans Publishing Co., 1969), 15.

2. Rebecca Pippert, *Pizza Parlor Evangelism* (Downers Grove, Ill.: InterVarsity Press, 1976), 12.

CHAPTER 2

Avoiding Evil Instead of Its Appearance

*G*et on the good side of how things work." Not bad advice... most of the time. The successful person finds out how things work, and then adjusts accordingly. He does not fight the system unless the system is wrong. Often it is.

Springtime was always a fun time when I was growing up at Aldrich Acres. Animal babies began to arrive, and their enthusiasm and zest for life was contagious. When we let the young calves out of the barn for their first exposure to the world of fresh air, sunshine, blossom-laden trees, and flower-filled pastures, they exploded. I mean they literally went insane. Their enthusiasm knew no bounds. But their world had boundaries called fences... electric fences. A wet nose on a hot wire shut down their scheduled frenzy for a moment, until they tried it again—*zap!* They didn't have to like the set-up, but they'd better get on the good side of how things work or the results were entirely predictable and rather shocking.

"Find out how Christianity works and then get on the good side of how it works. Don't fight it." Not bad advice, unless the "good side" is the wrong side. Christ called his followers to a radical life, a life which contradicted the expectations and the contrived boundary conditions of their religious practices. One of these expectations was to refrain from associating with certain "undesirables" based on appearance. Although Christ refuted this practice with his own life style, many today advocate this behavior as part of "avoiding the appearance of evil." Is this the right side, particularly when we consider what evangelism is and what going into all the world means?

CULTURAL CONFUSION

I've listed below some commonly held viewpoints within the Christian community. As you read through the list, ask yourself, Have these viewpoints been adopted because the Bible clearly teaches them or are they simply the views of a cultural Christianity? Many of the practices of Western Christianity are cultural. As such, they may be useful and effective. Unfortunately, however, many cultural patterns are counter-productive and actually work against the evangelistic enterprise—not to mention the truth of the gospel.

For example, in parts of Europe women with pierced ears are never allowed to take part in communion. The Bible nowhere rejects women with pierced ears as unworthy of communion. This viewpoint is clearly cultural, not biblical. Should we accept this provincial viewpoint as normative for the church at large, ignore it, or try to change it? What if I live in Europe and my neighbor with pierced ears has just found Christ? What a "joy" it will be to inform her that she is now a member of the church, the body of Christ, but can never participate in a communion service...ever. What fun it will be to share Christ with her equally "pierced" friend who has heard she is unacceptable because of something which transpired when she was eight months old!

The greatest barriers to successful evangelism are not theological, they are cultural. Many of our culturally determined patterns of life keep people from Jesus Christ!

Let's look at the list. Assuming that each statement is embraced by part of the Christian community, you decide whether its support is biblical or cultural. It's not always easy to determine.

Biblical Cultural

Biblical	Cultural	
❏	❏	Christians should meet together regularly for instruction andworship.
❏	❏	Christians should meet once a week before noon.
❏	❏	Christians should not be friends with non-Christians.
❏	❏	All Christians should stay out of taverns and bars.
❏	❏	Christians should study their Bibles on a regular basis.

❏ ❏ The pastor should run the church. He is the ruling elder.

❏ ❏ Wives should stay home and not work.

❏ ❏ A church board should rotate its membership every two or three years.

❏ ❏ Majority rule is the pattern for church leadership.

❏ ❏ Only elders can serve communion.

❏ ❏ Communion should be served only in the church.

❏ ❏ The non-Christian is the enemy.

❏ ❏ Women should wear hats in church.

❏ ❏ A collection plate should be passed each week.

❏ ❏ A Sunday school program is a must for the local church.

❏ ❏ An invitation to trust Christ should be part of every Sunday's program.

❏ ❏ Choir members should wear robes.

❏ ❏ The pastoral prayer should be part of the Sunday morning service.

❏ ❏ Christians should not smoke.

❏ ❏ The elder in a church should not drink too much wine.

❏ ❏ Every Christian should be a soul-winner.

❏ ❏ Pastors should speak from behind a pulpit.

❏ ❏ Christians should not be involved socially with non-Christians.

❏ ❏ Christians should avoid every appearance of evil.

❏ ❏ An elder should be one who is known for his love of strangers.

❏ ❏ Christians from other cultures who have more than one wife should divorce them all except one.

❏ ❏ Christians should not attend movies.

❏ ❏ What is wrong for one Christian is wrong for all Christians. There is no double standard.

❏ ❏ Legalism is wrong.

❏ ❏ Mature Christians are actively involved in the programs of the church.

❏ ❏ Midweek prayer meetings are a must for the local church.

❏ ❏ Prayer is part of the Christian's life style.

❏ ❏ Ashtrays should not be available in a true Christian's home

❏ ❏ Wine should never be found in a Christian's home.

❏ ❏ Christians should dress with modest, conservative styles of clothing.

❏ ❏ A mature Christian woman should avoid lipstick and makeup.

I spoke some time ago at a delightful conference in Switzerland. The local Christian community was upset when the American Christians brought Coca-Cola to the conference. According to them, "things may go better with Coke," but not if you're a believer. Imagine the confusion of a non-Christian who invited you over for dinner and you refused to drink his Coke. In the same way, many women who use cosmetics have been rejected because of cultural stigmas about wearing makeup. Fortunately, this is not as big a problem as it used to be.

Why do some believers get so upset when other believers drink Coke, wear cosmetics, enjoy bright clothes, watch TV, attend an occasional movie, associate with nonbelievers, and perhaps even have a glass of wine? Please understand, I am not advocating or rejecting any of these practices. I am simply asking a question . . . a question which has a direct relationship to evangelistic effectiveness.

FOUR POSITIONS ON DEBATABLE ISSUES

The conflicts I've described are the result of at least four positions Christians assume when a debatable issue arises. On any given issue a Christian operates out of one of four mindsets:

- Professional weaker brother;
- Susceptible weaker brother;
- Nonparticipating mature brother;
- Participating mature brother.

Pick a "gray area." Let's use going to movies to illustrate this difference. The *professional weaker brother* says no because it is sin for him and therefore sin for everyone. The *susceptible weaker brother* says no, because he doesn't think he has freedom, and may not know whether it is sin. The *nonparticipating mature brother* says no either because he does not feel he has the freedom or because he chooses not to exercise his freedom. If he feels he is not free and yet does it, he knows it is sin for him. Yet he recognizes and affirms the freedom of the *participating mature brother* to go to movies.

Issue		Evaluation	Conclusion	Possible Danger
1. Professional weaker brother	Movies	It is wrong for everyone	Everyone who participates is guilty of sin	Critical of other Christians who don't agree
2. Susceptible weaker brother	Movies	Probably wrong for him	It is not wrong for every Christian	Participation without full freedom of conscience
3. Nonparticipating mature brother	Movies	Either: 1) Sin for him, therefore he cannot participate 2) Not sin for him, but chooses not to participate	Believes that the same thing can be sin for one believer but not sin for the other	Can believe that the participating believer would be "more spiritual" if he would only limit his liberty
4. Participating mature brother	Movies	Believes he has freedom to participate	It is okay for him, but may be sin for others	1) Succumbing to the "professional" weaker brother 2) Causing the susceptible "weaker brother" to stumble 3) Abusing liberty

As the issue changes, so the positions held by individuals change. Probably no Christian is a nonparticipating mature brother on every issue. For parts of the European Christian community, drinking beer is not an issue. Those who have freedom before the Lord on this matter are participating mature brothers. At one time I was a professional weaker brother on the beer-drinking issue. Now I am a nonparticipating mature brother.

Now suppose that for a group of people beer is in, but movies are out. If movies are the issue, these believers can become professional weaker brothers (those critical of all Christians who go to movies), or they can become nonparticipating mature brothers (those who don't attend but are not critical of those who do).

Having seen the positions present within the Christian community, let's develop further some other reasons for conflict.

WHEN NONPARTICIPATION IS A PROBLEM

There are Christians who do not have the freedom before the Lord to engage in activities other believers enjoy. Paul reminded us of such people (Romans 14) . He makes it clear that until freedom to act is gained, they must refrain from certain behaviors even though other believers have complete freedom in the same area. This divergence creates tension.

Many of these brothers are not legalists. They are mature, nonparticipating believers. They accept their personal limitations in some areas but in no way try to make their limitations normative for the rest of the Christian community. They do not believe that their more prescribed and limited life style makes them any more spiritual than those with a greater freedom before the Lord. Obeying Paul's careful instructions to them, *they do not judge* the life style of the participating brother. These people, like all true Christians, get upset when there is a misuse and abuse of Christian freedom or when the Christian community refuses to deal with evil and impurity. However, they recognize that the Bible clearly teaches that there is a difference in believers' definitions of personal freedom.

But there is a class of weaker brothers who contribute to the problem because of legalistic attitudes. The legalist carefully builds his own pattern of living and then tries to make it normative for the entire Christian community. Spiritual maturity for one who thinks this way is finally achieved when he has closed all the right doors and cut himself off from all "evil." He has to ignore the spirit (the intention of the law) and major on the letter of it. And he makes other believers prisoners of his expectations. His mission in life is to be judge and jury for the rest of the Christian community. He is not weak in the biblical sense that his sensitive conscience will be injured by the actions of his liberated friends.

I call this "mature" believer who should know better the "professional weaker brother." He uses his misinterpreted "weakness" as a weapon to try to force others to comply with his viewpoint. From a biblical standpoint he is not weak if he is not susceptible. Despite this, he uses his alleged weakness to manipulate others. "Not infrequently it is the weak who is the real tyrant."[1] This form of hypocrisy contributes more toward the death of beauty in a church than any other factor. A person with this viewpoint needs to be confronted and rebuked with a desire to see him restored to the path of usefulness and blessing (Galatians 6: 1).

WHEN PARTICIPATION IS A PROBLEM

Another cause for the upset within the Christian community is the "stronger brother" (participating believer) who is not sensitive in the exercise of his liberty. This person becomes a crusader for liberty and in the process greatly damages the cause of true Christian liberty. Other believers who may be discreet in their use of liberty become footnotes for this person's arguments. This "stronger brother" may hinder and harm the genuine weaker brother. He also needs to be confronted and rebuked to restore him to usefulness and blessing. The mature believer acknowledges his legitimate liberties in Christ and then limits them when it is the appropriate thing to do. Liberty possessed does not have to be practiced. However, much greater effort has been expended to bind liberty than to liberate those who are truly in bondage.

The nonparticipating brother will not necessarily become more mature if he is able to exercise more freedom. His greatest growth step is probably attitudinal. He is balanced when he accepts and welcomes the participating brother as a legitimate and God-pleasing expression of spiritual maturity. He must banish all thoughts that the stronger brother would be more spiritual if only he would limit his rightful liberty.

Maturity for the participating brother does not necessarily involve the gradual limitation of liberty. If Christian maturity is equated with the life style of the weaker brother and excludes the case of the stronger brother, it is an illegitimate, unbalanced definition. The converse is also true.

WHEN EVIL'S APPEARANCE CAN'T BE AVOIDED

Another reason for turmoil within the church is the concept of avoiding every appearance of evil. There are life-style issues which must be avoided on the basis of this principle alone, even if there are no specific biblical directives. But in the majority of uses, this principle is misunderstood and misapplied. Before I develop this concept further, I want to make a couple of observations.

First, *it is impossible to act in such a way that we will be universally understood and accepted.* This is a basic axiom of life. Some people can't get off the fence. They fear rejection. They avoid anything controversial and numb themselves into oblivion. You can enjoy the safety of sitting on the fence only so long. Eventually it no longer matters. Even fence sitters will be misunderstood because motives are seldom discernible. Only God knows the heart, yet man often says he can discern the intention of other people. This he does by imputing motives (usually his own) to another person. To the pure all things are pure, but to the impure, pure things can be judged as impure.

Second, *it is inevitable that we will find ourselves on the wrong side of some man-made fences.* Like it or not, we will find ourselves trapped by cultural expectations in our churches. If we are considered to be on the wrong side of the fence, we either conform to those expectations or experience varying degrees of censorship and rejection. In some minds we have failed and are not living a Spirit-controlled life. According to them, we have not "avoided every appearance of evil."

Without making a moral (or emotional) issue of movies, let's suppose a non-moviegoing Christian sees his Christian brother going into a theater. The non-moviegoing Christian is offended because he believes theaters are evil places to be avoided. He confronts the moviegoer with the command, "Avoid every kind of evil" (1 Thessalonians 5:22). Is this a legitimate use of Paul's words? Does Paul mean we should never do anything that might look like sin to someone else? Did Christ follow this principle in his life?

In the previous verses, Paul is talking about prophetic utterances: "Do not put out the Spirit's fire; do not treat prophecies with contempt. Test *everything*. Hold on to the good. Avoid every kind of evil" (5:19-21). What is to be tested? The content, the message of every prophetic utterance. What is good is to be held on to; what is evil is to be rejected. The passage is *not* saying never do something which looks like sin to another person. Jesus Christ frequently offended the leaders of the religious community.

> They could not conscientiously approve the company He kept; He condoned law-breaking (was this not indisputably "sin"?) in allowing His disciples to gather corn on the Sabbath, or to pull an ox out of a ditch. He gained for Himself the reputation of the 'Prince of Evil' (Matthew 10:25, Phillips). [2]

Christ avoided evil of any kind, yet he did not always avoid the "appearance of evil." Jesus rejected the world's sinful structures and self-centered values, but he loved mankind, and in so doing was condemned by religious people. When the issues were nonreligious, Christ made every effort not to offend. He instructed Peter to pay the temple tax so that no one would have any reason for offense. When the gospel of the saving grace of Christ was at stake, when it was distorted by religious legalists, he confronted such distortions head on. He let his disciples eat with ceremonially unwashed hands although he knew it was offensive and divisive. He allowed them to pick and eat grain on the Sabbath even though this appeared evil to the religious community. He frequented "off limits" places and befriended unclean people. He was condemned for such radical behavior.

> His concern was to do the thing that pleased his father. If He could at the same time avoid offense, He did. If in being obedient, He at times horrified men of high reputation—indeed, of religious reputation—and appeared to be acting contrary to the law of God, He counted it of no consequence. [3]

Paul, too, vehemently resisted the attempts of the false religious leaders "to spy on the freedom we have in Christ Jesus and to make us slaves." Instead, he "did not give in to them for a moment, so that the truth of the gospel might remain with you"

(Galatians 2:4-5). When the issue of truth and the essence of the gospel were at stake, neither Jesus nor Paul had any hesitation about "the appearance of evil." Their lives and actions became carefully calculated theological statements which created controversy and generated accusations of every kind.

Christ deliberately chose to live a particular way and was accused of gluttony and drunkenness. Paul reprimanded Peter publicly for refusing to behave in a way that would have been offensive to the Jewish community. Peter knew that the gospel was for both the Jew and the Gentile, yet he refused to eat with the Gentiles for fear his behavior would "appear evil" to the Jews. Paul (rightly so) took him to the woodshed for it. The same Paul who wrote "Do not allow what you consider good to be spoken of as evil" (Romans 14:16) commanded Peter to dine with Gentiles whether the Jews spoke of it as evil or not. It should be noted that it was Jewish *Christians* who were offended!

Yet Paul cautions the believer to be sensitive to the weaker brother and guard against offense. The believer's behavior is not to destroy another believer (Romans 14:15). But it is not the *genuine* weaker brother who distorts the gospel by insisting on conformity to the culturally prescribed legalisms of an unbalanced Christian life style. It is the professional weaker brother—the self-appointed, rigid, unwavering, unstumbling, immovable, self-righteous individual—who often blows the whistle on Christians penetrating the non-Christian community with the gospel. To this person we must, as Paul, "not give in...for a moment, so that the gospel may remain" pure and undefiled in its simplicity and beauty. Succumbing to him makes me become bad news, a hypocrite, and a messenger of a distorted gospel.

LIVING IN THE TENSIONS

The perceptive Christian who has evangelistic effectiveness will always live with the tension between community penetration and the weaker brothers of the Christian community, whether genuine or professional. The combined pressures of the *expectations* of the professional weaker brother and the *immaturity* of the susceptible weaker brother may keep the mature believer from reaching non-

Christians with the gospel. If he knows before the Lord that he has freedom to entertain non-Christians, to socialize with them, to go into their homes, and to eat with them, but he fears the criticism and judgment of the professional weaker brothers, he faces continual tension and frustration. If he chooses to exercise his liberty and actually mix it up with nonbelievers, he will not avoid every "appearance of evil." He will be accused of eating with publicans and sinners and of breaking the established mores of the Christian community. He may even be accused of being a glutton and drunkard.

Sounds vaguely familiar, doesn't it. Wasn't there someone who was accused of the same thing nearly two thousand years ago? "If Jesus came back today and mingled with gamblers, the skid-row crowd and the cocktail set, a lot of shocked Christians would throw up their hands and say He was too worldly."[4] I guess he *was* guilty of being a friend of sinners.

Again, Christ must be our model. Christ is our great high priest who built a bridge between God and man. The Latin word for priest (*pontifex*) literally means "bridge builder." We as believer-priests are to also be building bridges as Christ did. He did not reject the caresses of a prostitute; he touched untouchable lepers; he scandalized the religious community by mixing with the riffraff. He was often where the beer cans and poker chips were present.

> We are to go as He went, to penetrate human society, to mix with unbelievers and fraternize with sinners. Does not one of the Church's greatest failures lie here? We have disengaged too much. We have become a withdrawn community. We have become aloof instead of alongside.[5]

AS RADICAL AS CHRIST

Can we be any less radical than Jesus Christ? The more a Christian is like Jesus—*really* like him—the more effective he is in evangelism. Christ said his life style wouldn't fit in old wineskins and therefore the prescribed, pharisaic, religious, pious, poker-faced platform was ruled out. Christ was characterized by a holy worldliness. This is the model for the believer. But it's risky; it's out with the wolves; it's dangerous. When sheep are out with the wolves, they must obey and trust the shepherd. But when they hang around the barn, who needs the shepherd? The tragedy in Christian circles is that often the greatest wounds come not from the wolves, but from other sheep. We need our Ephesians 6 armor to protect us from each other.

Why is it that we are the only army that shoots its wounded, as though to get wounded in battle was a sin? The sin is that so few are even *in* the battle. The few who make it to the front lines (through the barrage of criticism from their Christian comrades) and get wounded are often soundly scolded for going to the front lines in the first place. Clearly, it's safest to do nothing. But I know that's not what *you* want to do. Paul's whole point in discussing weaker and stronger brothers is a plea to recognize *how varied and diverse will be the behavior of those who are equally zealous in their commitment to please God.* In the light of this he gives some instructions in Romans 14, beginning with verse 10:

- "You, then, why do you judge your brother?"
- "Or why do you look down on your brother?"
- "Each of us will give an account of himself to God."
- "Therefore let us stop passing judgment on one another."
- "Let us therefore make every effort to do what leads to peace and to mutual edification."
- "So whatever you believe about these things keep between yourself and God."
- "Therefore do not let anyone judge you by what you eat or drink, or with regard to a religious festival, a New Moon celebration or a Sabbath day" (Colossians 2:16).

AVOID EVIL... NOT EVANGELISM

Here are some general observations and suggested principles for evangelistic effectiveness:

First, none of us is capable of fully understanding our own motives, much less those of another believer. Let's obey Paul and quit judging our brother. Such action is sin. God is the only one who sees your heart and knows your desires. He will judge you, not by someone else's standards, but by his own. That is both an encouragement (I am not answerable to my brother and his conscience) and a warning (I *am* answerable to God).

Second, beware of professional weaker brothers and be sensitive to susceptible weaker brothers. The Christian community has just as much responsibility to *educate* the susceptible brother as it does to guard against offending him. If a nonparticipative pastor fails to affirm the legitimacy of a more participative, penetrating life style, he is guilty of hindering the evangelistic effectiveness of the penetrating life style and perpetuating the susceptibility of the weaker brother.

We make it sound as though the information the susceptible brother needs to make choices is somehow unavailable. What does he need to know? He needs to know about morally neutral areas. All things are lawful (he has freedom); but not everything edifies or builds. He must learn about matters of conscience. One must not violate his conscience in the area of doubtful things. His conscience establishes his personal boundaries. As long as it is bound in a particular area, he is also bound. He must know that an action can be sin for him today (if he violates his conscience), and may not be sin for him a year from now (if he comes to a point of freedom of conscience in this area). He must recognize that freedoms vary with the individual. What is right for one Christian may be wrong for him; therefore, he must not allow the freedom of another to give him an excuse for sin.

He must be instructed about use and misuse of freedom. Some believers will misuse their freedom and set a bad example for him. Conversely, some will use their freedom effectively as a bridge to non-Christians. He must know how to use his freedom. His own liberty does not have to be exercised. He may need to limit it under certain circumstances. He must understand that liberty is contextual and situational. What is seen as liberty for one Christian community may be considered either license or sin in another. He cannot be bound by the collective conscience of the Christian world. Whatever he does in his context in one way or another will be considered wrong or imprudent somewhere else. Finally, he must know how to exercise his conscience. He must not bind others by his convictions. He must be taught to recognize and respect other Christians' freedom. It is the duty of every mature Christian person to educate the susceptible Christian. There is no reason for him to remain in this category for more than a short time.

Third, we must recognize and affirm the legitimacy of divergent life styles and learn to live with the tensions they create. Paul makes it clear that "meat eaters" and "nonmeat eaters" are both legitimate members of the body of Christ. "He who eats meat, eats to the Lord, for he gives thanks to God" (Romans 14:6). Eating meat offered to idols was offensive to some and nonoffensive to others. Some had freedom to eat it, others didn't. As a general rule, meat eaters make better evangelists. We will see why in a later chapter. Unfortunately, many churches have polarized around the nonmeat-eating life style and made it normative for all Christians. It has become *the* definition of spirituality. The healthy church affirms both meat eaters and nonmeat eaters and encourages them to live together in creative tension.

Fourth, we must not sacrifice truth to gain the approval of men. There was a searching community whose understanding of the gospel would have been distorted had Jesus or Paul succumbed to the pressures of conformity. There is a time when those who refuse communion because of pierced ears must be opposed because it is a distortion of the saving grace of Jesus Christ. There is a time when those who criticize believers who love, befriend, and associate with non-Christians must be opposed. They violate truth and distort the gospel when they parade their legalisms before others. There is a time when those churches who proclaim truth and produce ugliness must be opposed and rebuked because they mar the bride's beauty and present a caricature of Christ to the world.

Fifth, let's be certain we avoid evil. *Who* we are determines *where* we are. Not all are free to mix with non-Christians...but some are. Let's let them do it. The more mature we are in Christ, the better prepared we are to penetrate deeply and effectively into our non-Christian communities. The mark of true maturity is not withdrawal, it's penetration.

Sixth, as a general rule, the farther a Christian is from effective personal evangelism the more he is involved in criticism. Many in the church are like caged hunting dogs. With no birds to hunt they spend their time nipping, scrapping, and fighting with each other. Turned loose to fulfill their destiny, to pursue their quarry, to fulfill their great commission, they stop biting and fighting. There are more important things to do. I've tested this out, particularly with pastors. Inevitably the pastor who objects to befriending non-Christians has never befriended one himself.

Seventh, identifying with the world is not the same as being identical with it. As Rebecca Pippert puts it, Christ was effective because of his radical identification and his radical difference. His radical identification with the human race was totally out of character with the religious communities' expectations of God. Yet the reality of Christ's humanness called attention to his deity. It was often in the context of his similarity with mankind that his deity (his radical difference) came bursting through. Holiness and blamelessness make identification a safe enterprise. The disciplines of the Christian life are essential if identification is going to be *redemptive* rather than *destructive.*

Eighth, compromise is inevitable in life. As life moves on we discover that *some* of our dearly held axioms must succumb to the ax of maturity and truth. As a youngster I was convinced that no one who smoked was a Christian. Today I know better, and view such believers as brothers, although I still question the wisdom of their habit. One cannot live, work, or minister with another without compromise. Unity demands it. The carpet cannot be solid red, blue plaid, or forest green at the same time. Someone has to compromise.

Yet all of us must have absolutes we will not compromise. These absolutes are rooted solidly (and clearly) upon God's inerrant Word. Admittedly, the very word *compromise* is somewhat odious, but it is a necessary term. In youth, white is white, and black is black. Everything is so clear, so obvious. But age changes things. Age brings a new perspective so that we can see the necessity of compromise.

> When we are young, we refuse to compromise. When we are in our twenties, we see we have to compromise. When we are in our thirties, we are willing to compromise. When we are in our forties, we learn to compromise. Finally, we discover that compromise is what life is all about.[6]

In the words of Elisabeth Elliot, "Let us not be Pharisees in our certainty of what God could or could not permit." A bride is made of many parts, most of which are different in form, function, and purpose. To be beautiful, each part must be allowed to function properly, according to *divine specifications.* Let Christ build his church *and* judge its effectiveness. He as the Author of evangelism is the only one who can determine motives as well as methods.

A Christian must be sensitive to the problems and challenges posed by stepping across falsely imposed boundaries to share with others. He must be ready to enter another culture without rejecting it—but without selling out to it either. If he eats meat, he must not begin to worship the gods of the meat eaters. The next chapter tells how.

Notes

1. Anders Nygren, *Commentary on Romans* (Philadelphia: Fortress Press, 1975), 445.

2. Elisabeth Elliot, "What is Meant by the Appearance of Evil?" *Witness—Winnipeg Bible College* 56 (1978):3.

3. Ibid., 5

4. Leighton Ford, *The Christian Persuaders* (New York: Harper & Row, 1966), 12.

5. John R. Stott, *Our Guilty Silence: The Church, the Gospel and the World* (Grand Rapids: Wm. B. Eerdmans Publishing Co., 1969), 62.

6. Edward Dayton, "Compromise," *MARC Newsletter,* September 1978, 3 .

CHAPTER 3

Eating Meat and Evangelizing

Come with me on an imaginary journey into the home of a non-Christian neighbor. We are invisible. In the den, a *Playboy* magazine tops the stack of reading material on the coffee table causing a yellow caution light to flash on our spiritual dashboard. In the corner opposite a TV sprawls the man of the house, feet propped up, beer can clenched in one fist, TV remote in the other. The yellow light flashes again. Bob's tired from a rough day in the dog-eat-dog world. His mind is reliving the events of another day's scramble for the almighty dollar—a day of cutting corners, pressure, compromise, and more pressure. He's not entirely happy with what the realities of the marketplace have done to his boyhood ideals. But then, doesn't everyone have a price? He smiles when he thinks of his new Mercedes. Couldn't really afford it, but nobody needs to know. Besides, if he can close the Smith deal quickly, he'll make a killing. Isn't that what life's all about?

Glancing at his bookshelf, it's obvious that some of Bob's books did not come from the local library. Marian, the librarian, would have blushed. We don't blush—invisible people can't— but our yellow light continues to flash. Mom (Pam) puts down her cigarette long enough to answer the phone. She explains to the caller that they won't make the bridge party. They're going to a movie with some unexpected guests. The yellow light is at it again.

Sally, the teenage daughter, applies the finishing touches to her makeup. She has a date with her steady. They're going to a rock concert. She's on the pill. Yellow lights flash. Jim, Bob's son from a previous marriage, bursts into the den demanding his overdue allowance. His timing is poor. Bob shares with him a piece of his mind he can ill afford to lose. His complaints about Jim's hairstyle and earring add fuel to the fire. There are hard words. The air turns blue. Again, our spiritual dashboards light up. No grace is offered before the meal and there is little grace expressed during it.

But things calm down. Jim retires to his room. The rock star posters (not to mention the eastern guru's grinning portrait) do a number on our spiritual dashboards. The books on transcendental meditation don't help. It's a good thing we don't see the drugs stashed away under his mattress.

Responding to the doorbell, Bob welcomes Karen and Ned, friends from way back. Bob pours them drinks as they make small talk together. Karen and Pam disappear for a few minutes, providing Bob and Ned an opportunity to exchange some off-color stories salted with four letter words. Their boisterous laughter almost drowns out Karen and Pam's discussion of you, their next door neighbor.

They can't figure you out. You seem to enjoy going to your church and hearing someone preach at you. They shake their heads at the thought. It must be a terrible waste. And you wouldn't let your kids go to the ballgame on Sunday even though they really wanted to go. This they can't understand. Pam tells how they had offered to take your teenage son to the school dance, but you explained that you didn't allow your children to dance. That was okay, but your comments about being born again and accepting Christ and submitting to husbands didn't communicate. It's as though you had your own language. Your more Spartan, conservative life style doesn't go unnoticed either. It makes Pam feel somewhat guilty about her love of flamboyant, expensive styles. But what is wrong with looking good, eating good, and living good while it lasts? You can't take it with you. It must be a difference in values.

They consider your submission ideas a cop out. Your husband is viewed as a chauvinist, although he seems to be a nice guy. This "chain of command" stuff has to go. Pam says she feels you are in the dark ages intellectually. How can anyone believe that stuff about a virgin birth, miracles, and angels? Why would anyone involve herself with such an outdated life style? Pam knows you are better than she and admits she probably needs religion. In fact, she feels uncomfortable around you. They laugh together as she describes herself as your "project" in spite of her Christian Science background. Earrings finally in place, lipstick properly applied, they rejoin their husbands and drive off to laugh through an R-rated movie. Isn't this the good life?

CULTURE, CONVERSION, CONFLICTS

Why the yellow lights? Why the feelings of awkwardness and inadequacy? Because Christians are members of a new order, a new family with a redeemed set of beliefs, values, customs, and institutions. In Christ we are new creations and become members of a new culture. We are citizens of heaven. We are aliens, strangers, and pilgrims on this earth. It is not our home. We are different—radically different. Conversion has brought a radical change of allegiance. The new birth forces us to rethink our most foundational convictions. Our values, our entire world view, and our belief structure change.

We call the beliefs, values, customs, and characteristics of a particular group its *culture*. In a nutshell, culture is a body of ready-made solutions to the challenges, tensions, and problems of life. It is our emotional home, our mental furniture, an acquired way of coping. At the center of a culture is an understanding of the universe and man's place in it. This important world view may be theistic or atheistic. From it are established standards of behavior, values, and conduct. Within any given culture, there are numerous subcultures. For example, research indicates that within the world of hobos there are at least fifty distinct subcultures, each with its own language, attitudes, and customs.

Conversion involves "a transfer from one community to another, that is, from fallen humanity to God's new humanity."[1] This experience of being a "new creature" in Christ often causes great conflict. It is not unusual for a new Christian to reject everything associated with the past. Often he withdraws completely from his social environment, abandoning all previous webs of relationships. The radical nature of conversion makes it inevitable that it will strike at the root of the new convert's cultural heritage.

RESPONDING TO CULTURE

As the new believer grows in grace, his world view, his fundamental convictions, his values, his beliefs, and his social patterns must come under the lordship of Christ. All fundamental convictions must be reexamined. The Christian's response to culture is important because an understanding of culture is critical to effective evangelism. Throughout the history of Christianity the church has responded to the relationship between conversion and human culture in at least four ways.[2]

Rejection

The first response to human culture is *rejection*. This life style of withdrawal and isolation is not limited to monastic orders or religious sects. It is not uncommon among Christians in many of our churches.

> This "closed corporation" mentality, a sort of Christian isolationism, has been a constant barrier to evangelism. Many Christians have been so afraid of being contaminated by worldliness that they have avoided any social contacts with unconverted persons. As a result, they have no natural bridge for evangelism; what witnessing they do is usually artificial and forced rather than the spontaneous outgrowth of genuine friendship.[3]

Such rejectionists develop their own language, values, customs, and social activities. To them social segregation from the non-Christian world is normative. A *radical difference* must be maintained. The unbeliever is to be avoided at all costs. John Stott calls them "rabbit-hole Christians."

> You know—the kind who pops his head out of the hole, leaves his Christian roommate in the morning, and scurries to class, only to frantically search for a Christian to sit next to (an odd way to approach a mission field). Thus he proceeds from class to class. When dinner time comes, he sits with all the Christians in his dorm at one huge table and thinks, "What a witness!" From there he goes to his all-Christian

> Bible Study, and he might even catch a prayer meeting
> where the Christians pray for the nonbelievers on his floor.
> (But what luck that he was able to live on the floor with sev-
> enteen Christians!) Then at night he scurries back to his
> Christian roommate. Safe! He made it through the day and
> his only contacts with the world were those mad, brave
> dashes to and from Christian activities.[4]

An overstatement, perhaps, but not without truth. Because of
their emphasis upon *only* a radical difference, such Christians
have a message but no audience.

Immersion

A second response is *immersion,* the exact opposite of rejection. These Christians, sensing the need for a *radical identification*
with human culture, fail to maintain the radical difference so
important to the rejectionist. As a result, they become essentially
indistinguishable from the world. Their salt loses its saltiness and
effective evangelism ceases. They have an audience but no
message. These believers succumb to the world's pressures, allowing it to push them into its mold.

Split Adaptation

A third response of Christianity to culture is *split adaptation.*
This view is a blend of the rejection and immersion options. In
reality it is a form of spiritual schizophrenia. This person is a
citizen of two worlds and attempts to be at home in both of them.
Like the rejectionist, he strongly criticizes human culture as being
tainted by sin, transient, and without redeeming value. Yet he
adapts by conforming to the very world he denies. He drifts with
the majority opinion and experiences varying degrees of discom-
fort. The thought of bringing his faith to bear on the social ills and
injustices of his culture never crosses his mind. He has so compro-
mised the radical difference that it is neither radical nor different
any longer.

Critical Participation

The fourth response to culture is *critical participation.* A dual
citizen in heaven and earth, this believer knows that God has him
involved in a redemptive mission with cultural implications. He
does not believe that the new birth should "de-culturalize" a new

believer. Believers are to be spiritually distinct from the world's culture, but not socially segregated from it. The critical participator will face problems from the collision of the believing and nonbelieving cultures, however.

Paul faced the problem of conflicting cultural standards in Rome and Corinth. Some in the Christian community refused to buy or eat meat offered to pagan idols, while others felt freedom to buy and eat such meat. Conflict was inevitable.

Paul's answer to the problem was to the point. Both views were right, depending on the individual's conscience before the Lord. For one, eating was sin; for another, it was not sin. But the nonmeat eater had to remember that there was nothing inherently wrong with the meat because it had been offered to nonexistent deities. The conscience-stricken, nonmeat eater's response was correct in that he should not violate his conscience. And the meat eater had to be cautious, not because his actions were wrong, but because of the possibility of creating confusion on the part of the weaker brother.

All Christians are both meat eaters and nonmeat eaters, depending on the issue. Radical identification demands that in some amoral, neutral areas, we need to be meat eaters. Our Lord was, Paul certainly was, and we should be as we follow their example.

The critical participator lives with the perpetual tension between Christian faith and human culture. Although he is not deceived by promises of utopia on earth, he knows that he can be God's instrument to work in and through culture to mark men for Christ. His life mission is obedience to God and a loving concern for men. Surely our Lord would have us penetrate the world of government, school, work, and the home. Does he not also will us to penetrate those areas of modern life that all too often are lost provinces to the church: the worlds of the intellectual, of the entertainer, of the laboring man, of the disenfranchised?

We must maintain a balance between a critical transcendence (radical difference) and a concerned cultural participation (radical identification). If the vertical dimension is neglected, we face the temptation of becoming a cultural immersionist—a believer whose actions and thoughts are no different than those of a non-believer. If the horizontal dimension is neglected, we face the temptation of becoming a cultural rejectionist—a believer who has no identification with his society.

The key is to maintain a balance between our radical difference and our radical identification. Our radical difference is holiness (wholeness, not legalism or externalism). Only holiness makes radical identification a legitimate option for the Christian. At conversion, we usually move from cultural immersion toward radical difference. To become effective in evangelism we must move back toward our old culture, not to reimmerse ourselves but to become *radically* (and redemptively) identified with unsaved people. Although our Lord expects *communication* without *contamination,* we cannot communicate effectively without *contact* (identification). The following diagram shows the seesaw on which the Christian teeter-totters.

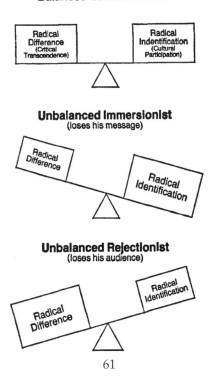

Balanced Communicator

Radical Difference (Critical Transcendence)

Radical Indentification (Cultural Participation)

Unbalanced Immersionist
(loses his message)

Radical Difference

Radical Identification

Unbalanced Rejectionist
(loses his audience)

Radical Identification

Radical Difference

There are dangers in trying to radically identify with our culture, however. The Christian who is highly involved with non-believers but minimally involved with Christian fellowship is in jeopardy. He has lots of identification but is in danger of neglecting those things which maintain a *healthy* radical difference. And he is in danger of being absorbed into a nonbelieving culture, thus nullifying his distinctive message.

On the other hand, the Christian who maintains a radical difference without a growing radical identification is likewise nullifying his distinctive message. He is being absorbed into a culture that does not exist outside of the body of Christ. He is so radically different from nonbelievers that no one except believers can identify with him.

DEALING IN THE BASICS

Let's pick up on a principle stated earlier. The greatest barriers to evangelism are not theological, they are social or cultural. Your neighbors, Bob and Pam, probably don't have a theological ax to grind with you. They just think you're sort of weird. They pick up some of the nuances of your radical difference and read it as rejection, especially if there is little or no radical identification. You get sweaty palms and have spiritual hot flashes when you are around them because of cultural differences. Having never experienced the radical change of allegiance to Christ, they don't embrace your values, talk your language, or support your customs and institutions. Consequently, yellow lights flash in your mind. Those effective in evangelism take the psychology and sociology of a culture seriously, accepting the tension it creates.

> It is only by active, loving engagement with local people, thinking in their thought patterns, understanding their world-view, listening to their questions, and feeling their burdens that the whole believing community…will be able to respond to their need.[5]

You may be thinking, "Okay, I accept that there will be tensions created by the differences between my culture and the nonbeliever's culture. How, then, do I bridge those cultural differences and become a wanted item (along with my message) by the nonbeliever?" The Greyhound Corporation once ran an ad which read "When you deal in basic needs, you're always needed." Exactly! How simple, yet how profound. When we as Christians deal in basic needs, we're always needed.

Love

The church as a bride is not to be a mannequin on display in a stained-glass bridal shop. Her beauty is dynamic and penetrating. The beautiful bride is not content to withdraw, obsessed with peace and tranquillity. She refuses to sit back and clip coupons on the spiritual investments of her forefathers in the faith. Love becomes her trademark as she deals in basic needs. It is *Christ's* love at work through the preaching, fellowshiping, worshiping, and serving of his bride.

Being a Neighbor

Love in Scripture has an interesting contextual bedfellow. It's spelled n-e-i-g-h-b-o-r. Loving your neighbor is part of the greatest commandment!

"Oh? But who is my neighbor?"

Nice try. Our Lord's answer to this ancient question makes it clear we cannot determine ahead of time just who our neighbor may be (Luke 10:25-29). Neighbors are to be loved. The Great Commission has not replaced the Great Commandment. A neighbor is someone in need who we can help. He may be beaten up and lying beside the road, but it's more likely that his wounds are carefully hidden behind a mask of adequacy. Our goal is not to determine who our neighbor is, but to be one. Most of us are neighbors to someone geographically, but few are neighbors to someone spiritually.

So what is a neighbor? The word *neighbor* comes from a root which means "to be near or close by." Therefore, *to be a neighbor is to develop the capacity to draw near.* "To draw near" presupposes distance. It suggests that there are obstacles to nearness. For example, the flashing yellow lights are obstacles to drawing near. The clash between the Christian and non-Christian subcultures is one of the biggest obstacles. Cultural shock is very real. But bear in mind that many distinctives of a particular Christian subculture are often cultural, not biblical. In most cases they are a blend of both cultural and biblical beliefs and values.

The effective evangelist draws near *in spite of* these obstacles. It is easy to see how false views of separation, professional weaker brothers, lack of social skills, opposition from believers, and just plain disobedience hinder our evangelistic impact. Evangelism that does not flow into the world of the unbeliever can become a raiding party, a foray into enemy territory, followed by a quick retreat to safety. How different this is from being a neighbor who loves.

The following list of potential distinctives underscores the problems of being a neighbor:

Unbeliever	Believer
• Nonbiblical world view	• Biblical world view
• New morality	• Marital faithfulness
• Materialist	• Not a materialist
• Drinks	• Opposed to drinking
• Ignores Christians	• Views non-Christians as the enemy
• Church peripheral	• Church central to life
• Honesty, integrity are relative	• Honesty, integrity are absolutes
• Swears often	• Never swears
• Made uncomfortable by Christians	• Told not to mix with worldlings
• Accepts culture	• Condemns culture
• Tries to appear perfect	• Tries to appear perfect
• Fears rejection by Christians	• Fears rejections by non-Christians
• Afraid of "conversion"	• Afraid of compromise
• Feels like a project	• Non-Christian a "project"
• Worries about what non-Christians think	• Worries about what Christians will think
• Enjoys dirty stories	• Rejects dirty stories
• Feels awkward	• Feels awkward, doesn't know how to relate
• Doesn't attend Christian events	• Doesn't attend non-Christian events
• Has no understanding of evangelical vocabulary	• Has a distinct evangelical vocabulary
• Kids in secular school	• Has kids in Christian school
• Possibly divorced	• Never divorced
• No biblical knowledge	• Basic biblical knowledge
• Comfortable in his non-Christian subculture	• Comfortable in his Christian subculture

PAUL'S EVANGELISTIC STRATEGY AND
CULTURE

We can learn much from the evangelistic strategy Paul used for the various cultures he ministered in. In 1 Corinthians 9:22 he writes, "I have become all things to all men so that by all possible means I might save some." Note how critical "becoming" is in the task of "saving some." To win the Jew Paul *became* a Jew. To win those under the law, he *became* like one under the law. To win some, he became all things to all men. In fact, he became a slave to *everyone* to win as many as possible (v. 19).

Becoming All Things

Evangelistic effectiveness is directly related to the ability to *become,* the ability to understand and relate to differences. To the Jew he became a Jew. To reach them he honored their noble institutions; he regulated his social life. He refused to blast his way through custom and conscience. He limited his liberty when it was appropriate.

To the Gentiles he did not appeal out of the Old Testament world view of the Jew. He didn't practice the Mosaic law among them or make it the basis of his preaching. It was totally foreign to their culture and life style. He tempered his brilliance and power when dealing with the weak. He never willingly insulted their beliefs and prejudices.

The issue at stake is not what I need to *know* as much as what I need to *become.* The critical question is not, "What *information* do I need to master?" as much as, "What *identity* do I need to assume?" The radical difference we have talked about must be biblical if evangelism is to be effective. To be radically different is not to be self-righteous, legalistic, and withdrawn. To be radically different is to be like Christ. This is our identity and the key to a redemptive identification.

Likeness Rather than Difference

Paul's efforts to adapt his life and method to the target audience underscore that every decision for Christ must be made within the framework of that person's culture if it is to be genuine. Paul's strategy focused on likeness rather than difference. We cannot expect the non-Christian to become a "cultural Christian" before he is a converted Christian. Whatever evangelistic strategy we use, it must fit the environment it is directed toward. Therefore we must understand our non-Christian neighbor and be willing to build bridges to him despite our differences in beliefs and values.

The areas of common interest do not have to be religious. If your neighbor is a fisherman, become a fisherman. If he's in the newspaper business, let him teach you about the newspaper business. I had the joy of influencing to Christ a friend who was an executive with the *Dallas Morning News.* I asked if he would mind giving me a tour of the operation. We spent one whole day together, and I asked every imaginable question. I took an interest in his world. I became a newspaper man. Soon he took an interest in my world, and became a Christian. A day in the oil fields with an oil company president produced the same results. I became an oil man, he became a Christian. With two of my neighbors I became a tennis player, and they became Christians.

PAUL'S PRINCIPLES OF CULTURAL SENSITIVITY

The same social and cultural flexibility exemplified in Paul must be encouraged within the Christian community. We need to take the risk of becoming culturally sensitive, while bearing in mind some critical principles.

A Flexible Conscience

First, Paul had a flexible conscience when it came to matters without moral significance. To relate redemptively one day to a Jew and the next day to a Gentile demanded such flexibility. Where cultures clashed, he undoubtedly violated Gentile sensibilities when he "became a Jew" and vice versa. Paul gives us a classic example of a legitimate, biblical, situational ethic. The ethical thing to do when eating with a Jew is to respect his dietary restrictions and order food that does not offend. Likewise, when eating with Gentiles, one should not insist on a kosher meal for fear of being hypocritical or offensive to the Jewish community. Remember that your definition of things "without moral significance" will probably be challenged by a weaker brother. Good judgment is the key.

In every situation, though, *a lost man's soul should have precedence over the opinions of some within the body.* This critical principle must be observed by all believers. If in becoming an oil man to win an oil man a believer finds another believer nit-picking, the oil man's salvation is more important than the believer's pettiness.

The goal is open communication so that no one imputes wrong motives or presupposes wrong desires. If you have a question, ask, don't prejudge. Things often aren't as they appear to be! Our goal is to maintain unity within the body, but not at the expense of truth or integrity.

A Sharing of Interests

Second, Paul was able to draw near because he made himself flexible to another man's interests, concerns, circumstances, opinions, and backgrounds. He transmigrated himself into their souls and clothed himself with their feelings, burdens, and concerns. He shared not only the gospel but his very life because the people became so dear to him (1 Thessalonians 2:8). He moved among people with the compassion of a nursing mother and the concern of an exhorting, encouraging father (1 Thessalonians 2:7,11).

A Server of Men

Third, Paul's whole life was a lesson in self-denial and servanthood. Visible self-denial activates powerful human instincts, especially when you are the beneficiary of it. Servants become irresistible...by divine design. Such self-denial begins in the mind: "Let this mind be in you, which was also in Christ" (Philippians 2:5, KJV). Christ did not consider his equality with God something to grasp. Instead, he "made himself nothing, taking the very nature of a servant" (2:7).

Paul wrote, "Though I am free and belong to no man, I make myself a slave to everyone, to win as many as possible" (1 Corinthians 9:19). Please note that there is no winning without serving. More about that later. He did not exercise his right to food and drink (9:4), to have a wife (9:5), or to receive a salary (9:12-14). Instead, he "put up with anything rather than hinder the gospel of Christ" (9:12). Paul's attitude toward life and people was foundational to his success. He willingly put up with anything to reach the lost. His commitment to Christ and to his redemptive purposes were unimpeachable. Every ounce of strength was directed to winning the lost by all possible means. To this end he beat his body and made it his slave (9:27). He said *no* to its many legitimate wants and desires. He was a slave to everyone to win as many as possible!

A slave functions to meet the needs of another. He becomes whatever is necessary to meet a need. Shoes need shining? He becomes a shoeshine boy. House need painting? He becomes a painter. Sickness? He becomes a nurse. Loneliness? He becomes a companion. A servant is sensitive to areas of tension, frustration, and imbalance, and then relates the gospel to a specific need. He finds that crack in the rim of the soul, that area of need for which the gospel becomes good news. Then he shares it.

EVANGELISM MADE EASY BY CULTURAL SIMILARITY

The easiest person for you and me to reach has three characteristics. He *has a similar cultural background.* It's generally true that the more I share in common with a nonbeliever, the easier he will be to reach. The easiest person to reach also *knows the essentials of the gospel.* The seeds of biblical truth have already been planted, perhaps in childhood. Finally, this person *has a good relationship with the evangelist—you.*

Your neighborhood undoubtedly contains some people with great cultural similarity. After you build social intimacy, you can speak from the platform of cultural similarity and social intimacy and share whatever knowledge is necessary for your neighbor to understand the gospel.

Everyone has a cultural imprint which must be taken seriously. Paul's example of "becoming" underscores the importance of a flexible life style that adapts to the individual and his cultural imprint. The point of contact between people and the good news is their need, hopes, and fears. But Paul became all things to *all* men so that he could win some. We should too. We must free ourselves to use our God-given creativity! Not only did Paul have an adaptable life style, he had a flexible methodology. He became all things to all men so that by *all possible means* he could win some.

> Before we criticize what the other man is doing, we ought to remember Moody's classic reply to a critic who disapproved

of his methods. "I don't like them too much, myself," he admitted—"what method do you use?" When the critic said that he used none, Moody tartly replied, "Well, I think I like the way I do it better than the way you don't."[6]

JESUS AND JOHN: DIFFERENT LIFE STYLES FOR DIFFERENT CULTURES

The comparison Jesus makes between himself and John the Baptist is an important illustration of the need for a diversity of *life styles and methodologies* (Luke 7). We should allow other Christians the freedom to adapt their life style or methodology to the culture they are trying to reach, even if those choices exceed the boundaries our conscience has set for us (assuming the issue in question is not a moral one). Let's look at Jesus' perceptive illustration in Luke 7:33-35.

> For John the Baptist came neither eating bread nor drinking wine, and you say, "He has a demon." The Son of Man came eating and drinking, and you say, "Here is a glutton and a drunkard, a friend of tax collectors and 'sinners.' "

Both John and Jesus preached a message of righteousness and both called men to repentance. Yet they were radically different in their life styles, even though both life styles were legitimate. Of priestly lineage, John had a right to wear priestly garments and enjoy rich food and drink. God had other plans for him: "John wore clothing made of camel's hair, with a leather belt around his waist, and he ate locusts and wild honey" (Mark 1:6). Hardly priestly food! Whatever John didn't do, Jesus did ("the Son of Man came eating and drinking").

But the Pharisees had reached a wrong conclusion from their observations of Jesus and John. John was not demon-possessed; he was filled with the Holy Spirit from birth (Luke 1:13-15). And though the Pharisees saw Jesus under all kinds of circumstances —including eating and drinking—they never saw him guilty of gluttony or drunkenness. Christ in no way abused the gifts of his Father. The Pharisees were right about one thing, though—Jesus was a friend of sinners. But there's no sin in that.

So what's the point? Two radically different life styles are contrasted. Both are necessary and both are legitimate. John the Baptist's life style was a condemnation of the religious institutions of the day. His life underscored the radical difference between the righteousness of the Pharisees and God's righteousness. The corrupt, indulgent, gluttonous priesthood lost sheep to a man who personified what a true priest of God should be. It was necessary for him to adopt an extreme life style to focus attention and make a point.

Although Christ confronted the Pharisees on occasion, his primary target was the common folks, the sinners. His strategy was to identify with them, to love them, and to be a physician to them. He entered into their culture while John withdrew from the priestly culture. John ministered from without as a prophetic voice. Jesus ministered from within as a shepherd and physician. If John the Baptist's life style was the only legitimate pattern for a Christian, surely Jesus would have "out-John-the-Baptisted" John the Baptist. If John drank no wine, Jesus would have drunk no wine, no Pepsi, no Coke, no RC, no Tab. If John ate no steaks from the altar, Jesus would have eaten no steaks, no locusts, no honey, no chicken, no eggs, no fruit.

But that's not what happened. John came not eating and drinking; Jesus came eating and drinking. Jesus mixed it up with unsaved people; John withdrew and became a desert recluse. The church which polarizes around either life style to the exclusion of the other is unbalanced. Meat eaters and nonmeat eaters must exist together in creative tension.

Both John and Jesus were evangelists. John was more proclamational; Jesus more personal. Not many Christians have the potential or opportunity to be involved in proclamational evangelism. We all should involve ourselves in personal evangelism. To do so effectively we must penetrate the culture of the non-Christian and become whatever is necessary for the gospel to become good news to our non-Christian friend. We must free each other to do this. Try being like Jesus! Like him, we must reach people where they are, using their language and meeting their needs. Adopting this life style of evangelism assumes that our gospel presentation includes our presence as well as our preaching. As we shall see, this life style involves a rethinking of our personal model of evangelism.

Notes

1. *The Willowbank Report: Report of a Consultation on Gospel and Culture,* The Lausanne Occasional Papers, no. 2 (Wheaton, Ill.: Lausanne Committee for World Evangelization, 1978), 20.

2. St. Olaf College Self-Study Committee, *Integration in the Christian Liberal Arts College* (Northfield, Minn.: St. Olaf College Press, 1956), 61-69.

3. Leighton Ford, *The Christian Persuaders* (New York: Harper & Row 1966), 71-72.

4. Rebecca Pippert, *Pizza Parlor Evangelism* (Downers Grove, Ill.: InterVarsity Press, 1976), 20.

5. *Willowbank Report,* 14.

6. Ford, *Christian Persuaders,* 68.

CHAPTER 4

Practicing the Presence in Evangelism

*A*n evening at the symphony can be a glorious experience. When you gather together a group of professional musicians, each gifted in the playing of a particular instrument, and they combine their talents to perform a musical masterpiece, you would be hard pressed to think of a more delightful experience for a music lover.

But I said "can be" because all of the ingredients are also present for a disastrous experience. If the symphony members refuse to play their own instruments and insist on playing the instruments of others—the violinists demanding to be in the horn section, while those in the woodwind section want to try out their abilities in the percussion department—you will probably witness a less than harmonious performance of Beethoven. And if each member prefers a different piece and a different composer, then you will undoubtedly listen to a rebellious mixture of discordant squeaks and sounds you will never want to hear again.

There is a great need in the Christian community for believers to utilize their individual talents and together play harmonious music that sounds forth the beauty of the gospel. When this becomes reality, the Christian symphony provides the background music, the accompaniment, for the individual soloist to play the music in his or her personal, private world. Evangelism then becomes effective.

Personal evangelism falls into one of three basic categories: 1) proclamational, 2) confrontational/intrusional, and 3) incarnational/relational. All three types are legitimate and used of God. But is it possible that one type of evangelism more effectively utilizes and maximizes the talents of each believer and at the same time presents the music more harmoniously?

PROCLAMATIONAL EVANGELISM

The early church was planted because of the strong proclamational ministries of the apostles. They preached on street corners, in synagogues, and in marketplaces. Certainly the gospel is a message to be preached. Although the proclamational approach to evangelism will have validity until Jesus comes, the majority of Christians will not reach their private world by this means. God has gifted a small percentage of his children to carry out this special task, and we need the Billy Grahams and Luis Palaus of this world and the pastors who also have this gift.

Most evangelistic services which gather nonbelievers in a listening, observing role fall into this proclamational mode. Generally the audience is passive and unknown to the evangelist. The methodology is evangelist-centered and, because of its large scale, basically impersonal. The exposure is brief...usually one or two hours. Countless thousands have found Christ through this God-ordained method, and Christians can be instrumental in seeing souls reached by bringing people to such services. Many do, and the results are obvious.

CONFRONTATIONAL/INTRUSIONAL EVANGELISM

The *confrontational/intrusional* model is probably the most common one. Generally the target audience is a stranger. The limited time factor makes confrontation an immediate concern, and because no prior relationship usually exists, intrusion is necessary before confrontation takes place. Witnessing to a stranger in the next seat on an airplane usually necessitates an intrusion into his thoughts and activities, and an intrusion (usually without invitation) into his private world of religious feelings. It means he must stop whatever he is doing and give his time and attention to a stranger. With the end of the flight approaching at an established time, the evangelist faces the dual challenge of first confronting a person's religious beliefs, and then confronting him with the reality of sin and his need for the Savior. This he must do as a stranger whose motives, integrity, and character are unknown.

Three things need to be said about this method. First, it is legitimate. Many have found Christ through such an approach. Second, it is limited. I doubt that 10 percent of the body of Christ will ever be effective in this type of evangelism. Third, it allows a much higher percentage of the body to meet unbelievers and give a positive witness with a little encouragement and training, especially if the believer does not feel it is necessary to dump the whole gospel truck. Sensitivity is the key. A good birth involves a healthy pregnancy. Most evangelism training programs focus upon a confrontational approach to evangelism. However, it is naive to assume that most people trust Christ as the result of a stranger witnessing to them during a one-time spiritual transaction. The vast majority do not. Furthermore, many are hindered from making a decision because of a bad experience with a zealous but insensitive witness. Much of the problem grows out of some false assumptions about the decision-making process. We will look at that later.

Training in this methodology is necessary. People do need to know how to say the words of the gospel. But sending these trained people out into strange neighborhoods as an ongoing program for evangelism can be unwise. This is true if there is no concern for the beauty of the corporate fellowship and no serious sending of the Christian into the webs of relationships in his own private world. Obviously, a church characterized by introspection and withdrawal has no other option. It is a neighbor-to-no-one spiritually. It has no capacity to draw near and in fact forbids it. Like John the Baptist's ministry it says, "You come to me," rather than, "I'm coming to you"…as a friend. Evangelism for those living in such an evangelical ghetto can be likened to a regular lowering of the drawbridge and a charge out into enemy territory, followed by a quick retreat across the moat.

How much more biblical to have a carefully nurtured church family whose members are released to be Christ's servants in their sphere of influence. The Christian loves his neighbor and evangelism becomes a byproduct of his self-giving love, not the reason for it.

> Just buttonholing a stranger, witnessing to him and pressing for a decision will likely do more harm than good. Most responsible people react negatively and often quite violently to such an assault. *It shows a fundamental lack of respect for human dignity and personality.*[1]

My greatest concern is not the inherent limitations of this approach as much as what it becomes a substitute for. It's like eating canned peaches all your life and never tasting a fresh one. All too often we put cut flowers in the hands of people instead of teaching them to grow their own plants. What a joy it has been for my wife Ruthe and me to see many of our neighbors become good friends and also trust Christ. They are born running and grow quickly because a follow-up matrix has already been established *before* they trust the Lord. We tie neighbor to neighbor in bonds of friendship. They trust the Lord and we all grow together.

> Much of present day evangelism is of the foster parent variety. The spiritual child is brought into the heavenly world by an outsider who then hands him over to a stranger who tries to bring him into a fellowship which is unfamiliar. Thus, at the start, the odds are against successful integration.[2]

Thank God for those dear saints who are out ringing doorbells on Tuesday nights. My intent is not to discourage them. These comments are directed to the 95 percent who are either incapable of such a ministry or feel they have no ministry in evangelism because the only visible model offends their sensitivities toward people. As a general rule, the confrontational approach should be considered an *abnormal* rather than a normal witness experience.

INCARNATIONAL/RELATIONAL EVANGELISM

In a new, unreached mission field, evangelism usually begins with *proclamation*, moves to *persuasion*, and then as decisions are solidified and converts grow, the gospel becomes a *visible presence.* But once a thriving church is established, the starting point for evangelism increasingly shifts from proclamation (confrontational evangelism) to presence (relational evangelism). When Christians live in an established community, they may still confront, but they can also relate. To relate is much more natural and less stressful. I also believe it is much more effective in the long run. Our goal is not to avoid stress—we're in a battle—but to increase effectiveness. We are looking not for the easy way but for the effective way.

Being a frustrated farmer, I like to think of evangelism as having three stages:

1. *Cultivation*—an appeal to the *heart* through the building of a relationship;

2. *Sowing*—an appeal to the *mind* through the communication of revelation;

3. *Reaping*—an appeal to the *will* in anticipation of a response.

Evangelism is gift-driven. Some are great cultivators. Some are gifted sowers. Others are gifted reapers. Furthermore, our Lord made it clear evangelism is a *process*. He told his disciples, "I'm sending you out to reap [stage three] what you haven't sown." Others had done the hard labor (John 4).

Reaping isn't the hard labor. Any farmer knows that. Breaking up the hard soil, pulling the thistles and thorns, and removing stone consume the greatest resources and demand the most effort. Cultivators should not feel guilty if they do not reap. Remember Paul's words, "I planted the seed, Apollos watered it, but God made it grow" (1 Corinthians 3:6). God is our joint-venture partner in this process of cultivating, sowing, and reaping.

Cultivation is what Paul meant when he said, "I make myself a slave to everyone, to win as many as possible" (1 Corinthians 9:19). No serving, no winning!

Peter Wagner likens cultivating (presence), sowing (proclamation), and reaping (persuasion) to three stories of a house. The decision process could be illustrated this way.[3]

The WORDS (logia) of the Gospel
- Conviction of Holy Spirit
- Encouragement of evangelist

REAPING (Persuasion)
FOCUS: Will
Reprise

Soul Winning
People who decided to act

- Bible reading
- Literature
- Mass media
- Sermon
- Personal sharing
- Home Bible studies

SEWING (Proclamation)
FOCUS: Mind
Revelation

Witnessing
People who heard the words (message of gospel) and understood their implications.

The MUSIC (ethos, pathos) of the Gospel
- Love
- Unity
- Good works
- Hope
- Social intimacy
- Acceptance
- Understanding

CULTIVATING (Presence)
FOCUS: Heart
Relationship

People who are helped and loved

Means of Evangelism	Steps of Evangelism	Results of Evangelism

Reaping is impossible without some kind of sowing. Evangelism involves both good works and good words. Sowing as used in this illustration can involve mass evangelism (Luis Palau), literature, mass media, or a personal confrontation. The sowing dimension of the evangelism process is absolutely essential. How can they believe unless they hear?

But sowing seldom takes place in a vacuum. A person listens because he's been loved. People don't care how much we know until they know how much we care. Clearly, the second story (sowing) rests on the first (cultivating). Cultivating involves both the corporate image of the church in the community *and* the life of the individual in relationship with the nonbeliever. It is interesting to observe churches filled with new believers even though there is little or no overt emphasis on individual evangelism.

> The key seems to lie in the fact that the body is healthy and growing as intended, without evangelistic frenzy. In such situations, the body itself, collectively rather than individually, is having a distinct evangelistic result. This appears to be far closer to the norm for the church than some of the grand strategies of outreach being practiced today.[4]

When those who possess the nature of God begin to *express* it, cultivating builds and the stage is set for sowing and reaping.

Cultivating establishes the validity of what is proclaimed. Relationship alone is not enough. No one is good enough to let just his life speak for Christ. Words are necessary to point beyond himself to Christ. Nevertheless, the unbeliever needs to *feel* the impact of the good news that Christ loves people, and not merely listen to it. When love is *felt* the message is heard. But relationship which never leads to sowing is an extreme to be avoided. We are fishers of men sent to catch fish, not frogmen who swim with the fish, making our presence known. A healthy relationship increases the impact of the gospel's revelation because it helps people to perceive the gospel as good news.

Confrontational evangelism usually bypasses the first story and begins at the second. If a person experiences the second story without a healthy first story, he will normally interpret it as a confrontation or intrusion. He may make a decision, but often it is because of manipulation, fear, or the desire to get rid of the evangelist. When a stranger is the spiritual midwife, healthy follow-up is less likely.

EVANGELISM FOR ALL

As the missionary efforts of the apostles spawned churches, there was a subtle shift in evangelism strategy. Evangelism became more relational as the gifts of the body were brought on line for service. A study of the verbs used in Acts and then later in the epistles illustrates this shift of emphasis. The incarnational/relational method simply takes the cultivating, sowing, reaping model seriously.

This is the approach the majority of Christians can use with great effectiveness. There are at least seven good reasons why.

First, the incarnational/relational method does not require lots of biblical knowledge. What you know is not as important as what you are. *Second,* it is truly personal evangelism in that it deals with persons not strangers. *Third,* its effectiveness is directly related to the exercise of *all* the gifts of the body, not simply the gift of evangelism. God can use the gift of helps to win someone to the Lord. Someone's gift of administration might be God's channel of grace for a searching heart. Another may hear the music for the first time through a home-cooked meal made available in time of need. The gift of wisdom can become redemptive as another believer, having won the confidence of a friend, is able to listen and guide him through a problem. The gift of hospitality has explosive evangelistic potential...if it ever includes non-Christians.

A *fourth* reason the incarnational/relational method is effective is that it frees the Christian from unnecessary (and often unbiblical) pressure. His primary calling is to witness, to be a light, to play the music. His strategy is low pressure, long range. He is a seed planter who knows when to plant the seeds! He thoroughly trusts God to bring a harvest. This does not mean he is lazy. It simply means he knows you have to plant seed, cultivate it, water it, and wait for the harvest. *Fifth,* this model builds the context for meaning. A basic communication premise is that *nothing has meaning without context.* The *content* of the gospel (the words) gains added impact when it is communicated against the backdrop of the *context* of the gospel (the music). *Sixth,* it usually means that at some point a person will have to share the words of the gospel. Cultivation can take a person only a limited distance toward the cross. But if cultivation is really felt, and is positive, the unbeliever will ask you the reason for your hope! Believe me, it happens.

A final reason for the success of the relational approach is that it allows you to build the foundation for follow-up before nonbelievers come to Christ. By involving yourself in various neighborhood events (such as holiday gatherings, block parties, Cub Scouts), webs of relationships develop. As we will see later, it is out of these relationships that people come to Christ. Friends trust Christ and are followed up by a friend. That's New Testament evangelism!

This method does not exclude the confrontational approach. We do have a responsibility to witness to strangers in a responsible manner, a subject I will take up at the end of this book.

ESCAPING IRRELEVANCY

Before looking more closely at the differences between the incarnational/relational and the traditional models of evangelism, we need to pause and underscore a crucial fact with a crucial implication. Our world has changed. It keeps on changing. Sometimes the implications of change escape our notice. One major implication is that our presentation of the gospel must adapt itself to a vastly changed target audience. It is not a question of changing the gospel. It is simply recognizing that the people it is addressed to are not the same. We do not need to make the gospel relevant. It is. Sometimes we aren't.

Many forces add to the Christian messenger's growing irrelevance in today's world. Most non-Christians have no conscious awareness of the Christian faith. Secularization has gradually eroded a Protestant ethic and world view which formerly was passed on from generation to generation. When Dietrich Bonhoeffer wrote that the world had "come of age," he was declaring that man no longer considered God to be a necessary hypothesis to explain man and his world. Today many are totally ignorant of the most basic assumptions of the Christian faith.

Another large barrier is the non-Christian's lack of understanding of the most simple Christian terms. Heaven, hell, saved, lost, born again, redeemed, and other such evangelical buzz words used to be pretty well understood by the majority of our culture. That is no longer true. By and large, the language of the gospel is a foreign language.

Because there has been such an erosion of the gospel's fundamental truths and such widespread misunderstanding of its application, there is not much of a felt need for it today. Also, it is not true that the average unsaved person is desperately searching for answers to life. More often than not, he is generally satisfied with life.

> Some object that people cannot be happy without Christ, but such a viewpoint is naive. Remember that happiness is a relative thing—people are happy *given the light they have.* Furthermore, it will be difficult to convince them to the contrary, because those who are happy and satisfied are a nonresponsive segment with closed fetters.[5]

The rapid pace of life, a shrinking globe, the rise of technology, and the more transient patterns of life have created a growing sense of alienation. And the fewer the roots geographically, socially, emotionally, or spiritually, the fewer the needs felt for the gospel. Finally, emotion-tugging appeals are rationalized away as irrelevant. Appeals designed to create a response by playing on guilt are generally not as effective as they may once have been because guilt is explained away. Only a vague doubt lingers. These and many other reasons combine to press upon the Christian messenger the stamp of irrelevancy. This can be avoided if we are willing to change the presentation—not the content—of the gospel.

DEDUCTIVE AND INDUCTIVE EVANGELISM

Traditionally, evangelism courses teach people one basic approach to witnessing. They are trained to announce a blanket gospel message suitable for all. George Hunter calls this approach a deductive model of evangelism.

> It takes many forms, generally emphasizing three stages. (1) The witnesser announces a general gospel to the person with whom he is sharing. (2) The witnesser appeals to this person for an umbrella commitment to the general gospel that has been shared. (3) It is presupposed that if the person accepts this general gospel, he or she will work out the implications of this commitment throughout his or her life.[6]

A vacuum cleaner salesman using a deductive approach would run through the standard sales pitch even if the lady had no carpets. He would shampoo her floors and vacuum her nonexistent drapes. Turned down, he would go to the next home and repeat exactly the same pitch, with a similar disregard for the individual differences (and needs) of his audience. The opposite of general (deductive) is specific (inductive). The general approach to evangelism is increasingly ineffective in a pluralistic society with such a wide diversity of biblical background and understanding.

The inductive model presupposes knowledge about the individual being addressed. The gospel is then tailor-made to his individual needs. The goal is to discover that point in his life at which the gospel will become good news, and then to proclaim it. Jesus' method of dealing with people followed this adaptive, inductive model.

> To Nicodemus the ruler, he said, "You must be born again" —he never used "born again," a highly conceptual metaphor, in any other recorded instance in the New Testament. He talked to the woman by the well about "living water." But when the rich young man came up and asked what he had to do to have eternal life, Jesus did not talk to him about living water. Knowing that money was this man's god, he said, "Sell your possessions and give to the poor, and you will have treasure in heaven. Then come, follow me." He was basically calling him to a total switch of Gods. On the other hand, he didn't tell Zacchaeus, the tax collector who went up in a tree, to give away everything he had. He simply said, "Zacchaeus...I must stay at your house today." By the end of the day, Zacchaeus had decided on his own to give half of his possessions to the poor.[7]

Jesus met a person at his point of need. We should too. If his need is in his marriage, God has good news for him. If he is struggling with guilt, God has good news for him. Likewise God has good news for the person who needs love and affection, security or esteem. A confrontational/intrusional model of communication will be more general (deductive) because the individual being evangelized is virtually a stranger. Unfortunately, many people have had bad experiences with the deductive approach and have become virtually immune to it. A caring friend who meets them with the gospel at a point of need is often the only way they will see through the caricatures to the real Christ. The inductive method is a process which begins with the specifics of the individual's life. During the process, the evangelist finds himself doing at least five things:

> 1) *Relating* to the unbeliever's humanness and uniqueness with a view to helping him solve a problem.
>
> 2) *Discovering* the nonbeliever's problems and needs for which the gospel will prove to be good news.
>
> 3) *Sharing* how the gospel relates to that felt need and ultimately solves his real need.
>
> 4) *Advocating* a commitment which will make the gospel solution operational through the Holy Spirit.
>
> 5) *Supporting* the unbeliever's feelings and thoughts as he moves through the commitment process.

What do I do to win my friend for Christ? I focus on him as a person with a view to relating the good news to a need in his life. To do this I enter the process pictured above. At any given time I am operating out of one of these five postures. The process may go on for months or for only a few hours. The timetable, however, is not as important as the process itself.

DISCOVERING NEEDS BEFORE SHARING SOLUTIONS

It is important to think like a naturalized citizen of the unbeliever's world. He does things for his reasons, not yours. Research reveals that "people will not listen to the gospel message and respond unless it speaks to *felt needs.*"[5] Felt needs are the starting point for communication. From this base the Christian witness moves to sharing Christ as the solution to the unbeliever's real need. Meeting felt needs is often the key that unlocks the opportunity to share Christ.

Effective evangelism begins where people *are,* not where we would like them to be. As the King's messengers, our challenge is to help others discover how their needs can be satisfied through a relationship with Jesus Christ.

Ultimately, the purpose of evangelism is to help someone solve a problem...a critical problem which is literally a matter of life and death. It is common knowledge in the sales world that people do not buy a product because they understand the product; they buy a product because they believe a salesman understands them. The expert salesman must be a *people expert* as well as a *product expert.*

Many Christians know their "product" (the gospel), but they don't know people. Christians need to think through what the gospel can mean to a searching heart. Besides deliverance from a literal hell, it may put an unbeliever's marriage back together, it may end his overpowering guilt, it may free him from a burdensome habit, it may bring peace, it may bring financial stability, it may solve many of his interpersonal problems, it may be the key to coping with illness, it may be the solution to a tragedy or some great loss, it may be the key to resources for living. Possibly it will be all of the above. That's good news! Every basic human need or motive is matched by some facet of the gospel.

I find Maslow's hierarchy of needs helpful, though not foolproof, in determining what level of need a person is struggling to satisfy. If I can link a solution (the gospel) to a felt need, I have created a favorable climate for action. If I'm hungry, I'm motivated to meet that need. My thoughts and desires turn to food. If my need for food is acute, all other needs are subordinated to this need. As long as any need is not satisfied, a problem exists which seeks a solution. Maslow believed that all men have basically the same set of needs and attempt to satisfy them in a definite order of importance, beginning with the bottom of the pyramid and moving upward.

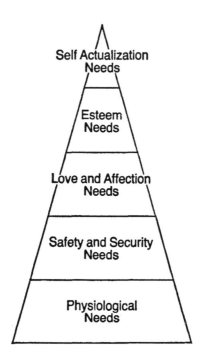

Maslow believed that although all of these needs are intrinsic to the human family, not all of them are on center stage at the same time. What a person says he wants is generally related to his basic need. A person may say he wants a new home or a vacation to Hawaii. If you ask him why, you will be much closer to discovering what basic need he is trying to satisfy. He may want a Mercedes because he has a deep-seated esteem need. He is unsure of his identity and feels a Mercedes will enhance his image and increase his esteem.

Man's most basic needs are *physiological:* food, shelter, clothing, and warmth are examples of physiological needs. For a starving man, his consuming focus is food. While it is true that "man does not live by bread alone," *if he has no bread he doesn't live at all.* Thank God for World Vision and other Christian organizations involved in meeting this need worldwide. Heaven for a hungry man is a place where God sits him down to a table groaning with food. It was Gandhi who said, "Even God cannot talk to a starving man except in terms of bread." Those who enter the millennial kingdom are those who have demonstrated the reality of their faith by feeding the hungry, giving drink to the thirsty, housing strangers, clothing the naked, tending the sick, and visiting those in prison (Matthew 25:34-36). The first good news for a starving man is bread, which will hopefully lead him to the Bread of Life.

Once physiological needs are met, a person seeks ways to meet his *safety needs.* Our need to feel safe and secure runs deep. We all want to be free from fear and anxiety. Most of us do not face constant threats to our physical being. Inflation, depression, and social and political unrest are more sophisticated threats. Man's inability to explain his origin and destiny is another threat to security. Fear can be a reason we trust Christ. Many come into the Kingdom because of a deep-seated security need. For the insecure person, the good news of the gospel provides an eternal security which tempers all temporal insecurities. Heaven for an insecure person is a place where he rests secure in the arms of one who forgives and welcomes prodigal sons and daughters.

But not everyone has a deeply felt security need. If a person is basically secure, his efforts focus "upward" to satisfy the need for *love and affection* in meaningful relationships. People have a desperate need to belong, but sin has blown all our circuit breakers and moved every relationship toward separation and concealment. We need a physical and emotional home in which our brokenness is accepted. Does the gospel have any good news for the person struggling with a love and affection need? Many come into the Kingdom through this door. The woman taken in adultery prostituted her body to get love and found only humiliation and disillusionment (John 7:53-8:11). The members of her sorority are legion. Jesus' love, understanding, and acceptance were what she needed and longed for. She just didn't know it existed. Many don't.

Every person needs to feel he or she is valuable and important. We all struggle with *esteem needs.* We want others to feel we have contributed something worthwhile to life. We all need affirmation from others. Yet there is no better news than to discover that I am a somebody to God. He knows my name and I am special to him. Do you know a non-Christian, starved for recognition, who is struggling with this need to feel valuable? Friend, have you got good news for him! Maybe if he feels he is valuable and worthwhile to you, God will use that as a stepping stone to Christ.

When the individual's need for esteem is basically met, he mobilizes his time, energy, and resources to become as much as he can be. *Self-actualization* is the need to realize one's inner potential by fully developing his capabilities. That this need for achievement is never fully satisfied is especially frustrating for the non-Christian. Hoping to fill a God-shaped vacuum with personal achievement doesn't work. Thousands of "successful" people suffer from destination sickness. They've arrived...empty. They need a worthwhile purpose which links their achievement to something beyond their own self-interests. They need to know that it is possible to achieve and receive eternal dividends. Many would be delighted to discover that there is the possibility of hearing the Lord of the universe say, "Well done, good and faithful servant." Maybe we should tell them.

USING MASLOW'S HIERARCHY IN EVANGELISM

This diagram of needs, though but a tool, does provide some helpful insights for finding needs and relating the gospel to them. The preacher or evangelist can use it as a grid for studying a passage. He should ask himself how the text might meet the needs of people struggling with one of the various need levels. What does it have to say about security, about love and affection, and so on? A sensitivity to these needs can greatly improve his communication (sowing), especially if he realizes he, too, is working out of a need level that may color his interpretation of Scripture. Maslow's model also lets us see how important genuine Christian fellowship can be as it is targeted to meet these needs. Need-centered fellowship stimulates the church to be a healing communion where we can experience security, love, acceptance, esteem, and self-actualization. The serving dimension of church life can be expanded if these basic human needs are understood and met. As you study the following chart, notice how man's needs are opportunities for us to share God's solution. People are more inclined to respond to the gospel when they understand how trusting Christ will satisfy their needs.

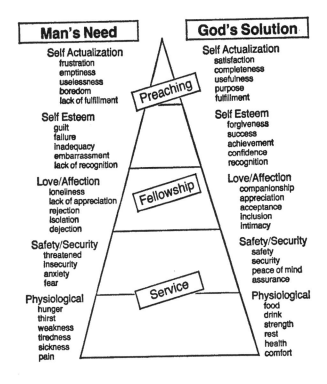

George Hunter suggests two furthr refinements which are full of insight. Those near the top of the hierarchy of needs are generally the stronger, more adequate people. Those at the bottom are the weaker, more vulnerable ones"

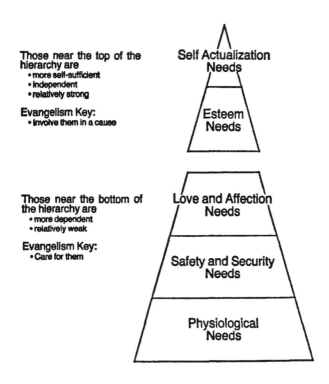

Those near the top of the hierarchy are
• more self-sufficient
• Independent
• relatively strong

Evangelism Key:
• Involve them in a cause

Self Actualization Needs

Esteem Needs

Those near the bottom of the hierarchy are
• more dependent
• relatively weak

Evangelism Key:
• Care for them

Love and Affection Needs

Safety and Security Needs

Physiological Needs

Traditionally, the church has ministered more effectively to the "down and outer" than the "up and outer." The person struggling with hunger, safety and security, or belonging needs is most easily reached by the church's care and love. Therefore, evangelism has generally targeted these needs and not the higher ones.

One's position on Maslow's hierarchy is never secure. A stroke, death of a loved one, or a financial reversal can render a strong man weak in an instant. The Christian's job "is to find people where they now are on the hierarchy of motives and to engage them at the appropriate level."[10]

To evangelize the weak, we come to find and meet a need. To reach the strong, self-assured person, we involve him in meeting *someone else's need.* We all have a great need to have something to live for. Get the strong person involved with Christians in some type of mission or serving activity. Let him feel something of the heartbeat of redemption as he involves himself in a worthy cause. As he gets successfully involved with other Christians, he will be inclined to accept the Christian's goals and values before he even knows them. I've had non-Christians host Bible studies, and they eventually came to Christ. Painting projects, providing transportation, raising funds for the needy, taking food to the ill, refurbishing a widow's house—the possible projects for involvement are unlimited. Take your neighbor along the next time you have a work day, especially if he has a special skill that can meet a need.

Paul became all things to all men so that by every conceivable means he could win some. God grant that we will do the same! Begin by being a friend, one who builds bridges not barriers. Camp close to needs and pray that God will allow you to be part of their solution.

Notes

1. James Jauncey, *Psychology for Successful Evangelism* (Chicago: Moody Press, 1972), 123.

2. Ibid., 61.

3. Chart adapted from Peter Wagner, *Frontiers in Missionary Strategy* (Chicago: Moody Press, 1971), 134.

4. James Engel, *Contemporary Christian Communications* (Nashville: Thomas Nelson Publishers, 1979), 217.

5. Ibid., 126.

6. George Hunter III, *The Contagious Congregation* (Nashville: Abingdon Press, 1979), 38.

7. Leighton Ford, *Good News Is for Sharing* (Elgin, Ill.: David C. Cook, 1977), 90.

8. Engel, *Christian Communications,* 117.

9. Hunter, *Contagious Congregation,* 45-47.

10. Ibid., 46.

Part 2

Evangelism and the Local Church

Evangelism and the Church Member

*T*he world listens when Christians love. Consequently, the corporate image of the local church in its community is a critical factor in its evangelistic impact. "In the final analysis, *the church is both message and medium, exemplifying and proclaiming the kingdom of God."* [1] This truth has tremendous implications. "At the very least, it is obvious that the church not exemplifying the kingdom is moribund and ineffective in the cause of world evangelization." [2] Our world is full of professing Christians who claim to believe the truth, but are producing ugliness. They can't get along. They fight, gossip, and often act like they were weaned on dill pickles. Instead of being an ambassador in the world, they are an embarrassment to the world. They'll fight for the "truth," but have *no* grace. The edification process has somehow broken down.

THE PLACE OF EDIFICATION IN EVANGELISM

The body of Christ, like a living organism, is subject to disease. If disease goes unchecked, the bride is weakened and fails to display God's beauty. Israel stopped growing and became a harlot. Her beauty declined as individuals shifted their loyalties to ungodly priorities and neglected spiritual disciplines. A gradual erosion of faith led to disobedience and sin. Spiritual adultery took its toll. A body of believers cannot remain in neutral very long. It will move either toward holiness or harlotry, toward beauty or prostitution. Persistent, consistent edification is God's antidote to spiritual prostitution.

When the body functions properly, it "builds itself up in love" (Ephesians 4:16). This process of edification brings the implications of the good news into contact with every facet of life so that it may be redeemed or set free for usefulness. Edification involves a renewal of the mind, bringing into captivity every thought so that it relates to Jesus Christ.

As edification takes place, I become increasingly Christ-like. Attitudes begin to change, relationships are healed, new relational skills develop, negative character traits and habits begin to disappear. And I become a more positive, attractive, Christ-like person. If evangelism is accurately expressing what I possess in Christ, then *edification* is the key to *evangelism.*

Evangelism as a way of living begins with believers who make beauty a way of life. If I am serious about beauty, I must be serious about the church; not only is it the bride (we hope a beautiful one), but it is also the beauty parlor. Built into the church by God are all the helps, all the dynamics, and all the resources you and I need to move toward wholeness. The wider our exposure to the giftedness of a properly functioning body, the greater our potential for beauty.

Therefore, we will consider the biblical principles a healthy church is built around. " 'The issue,' says Orlanda Costa, is not 'how many Christians can be enlisted for action or how the church "saturates" society with the gospel, rather it is how we get the dynamic organism to grow internally.' "[3]

There are two important reasons why anyone developing an evangelism strategy must first look at the health of the body. First, *God is not in the business of putting healthy babies in malfunctioning incubators.* Churches must become candidates for God's blessing. The theologically orthodox church at Ephesus was warned by God that if she did not recover her love, he would remove her candlestick (put her out of business). This is where the vast majority of evangelism training courses fail. They focus on training a small minority within the church to evangelize and do nothing to bring the majority of the believers into a state of health and beauty. Those converts the special task force wins to the Lord often find assimilation into the body very difficult, because beauty has not been taken seriously.

Second, the health of the body is critical to effective evangelism because *personality is a product of relationships.* We become like the people we associate with. The evangelist going door to door reflects the values, attitudes, and actions of his peers. When I counseled at a summer youth camp, I was amazed to observe how the campers copied their heroes. If they thought I "hung the moon," they would soon talk the way I talked, walk the way I walked, and develop similar manners, gestures, and vocabulary. They were becoming "little Joes."

We all are "value vacuum cleaners." Our values are shaped by our associations. This principle works both ways. If we treasure friendship with a person or group, we tend to become more and more alike as we shape and reinforce each other's value systems. On the other hand, if we strongly dislike a person or group we tend to reject their values, whether right or wrong. Thus our values, which influence the choices we make, are socially anchored. In Luke 6:40 our Lord reminds us that "everyone who is fully trained will be like his teacher." Notice it doesn't say "he will know what his teacher knows." He will be *like* his teacher— good or bad, beautiful or ugly.

In 1 Thessalonians 1:5 Paul says, "You know how we lived among you for your sake." He calls attention to an *intentional* lifestyle. He is saying, "We chose to live a certain way while we were among you." In the next verse Paul says, "You became imitators of us." He lived *intentionally* because he knew he was their model; they would become like him. In like manner, Paul encourages Timothy to "continue in what you have learned and have become convinced of, because you know those from whom you learned it" (2 Timothy 3:14). In verses 10 and 11 he portrays what it was that Timothy knew about him: "You, however, know all about my teaching, my way of life, my purpose, faith, patience, love, endurance, persecutions, sufferings." Timothy, like the church at Thessalonica, was an imitator of Paul, who lived intentionally among them.

The result of the Thessalonian believers' imitation of Paul's life style is given in 1 Thessalonians 1:7—"And so you became a model to all the believers in Macedonia and Achaia." Paul's leadership model was imitated by one church and then became the model for many other churches. Church leaders who are serious about evangelism must see the principle of modeling as crucial to the impact of their local fellowship.

The character of our churches is also cast in the mold of our associations. We are in large measure the products of the people we value and fellowship with. If "God's frozen people" accurately describes a local church, visitors and members will ice skate down the aisles *together.* A frigid church neither produces warm people nor attracts nonbelievers. The "belief of truth" is not synonymous with beauty. Many "believe the truth" but produce ugliness. Our dominant attitudes, thoughts, and beliefs determine our actions. If negative, legalistic, critical, cynical attitudes characterize the church fellowship, then it is likely that these attitudes are owned by the individual members.

THE PRODUCTS OF HEALTH

Lloyd Ogilvie has come up with five key questions which underscore the importance of the corporate fellowship of the church for evangelism. The rest of this chapter will develop an answer to his first question about the health of the body's members.

What kind of people does the church want to deploy into the world? What is our product? "No one responsible for helping another to grow spiritually can proceed until they have in mind a model of the outcome of their efforts."[4] Yet I am amazed to discover that most pastors and church leaders have given little thought to this critical question. Imagine a businessman renting a building, purchasing machinery and material, hiring employees, and then turning them loose to produce whatever they desired. No, there has to be a product design, an idea of the intended result. If believers are to be salt, lights, ambassadors, witnesses, and living epistles all rolled into one, what will "epistle readers" be given to read?

What is the biblical profile of a healthy member of the second incarnation? As lights who make visible the invisible attributes of God, the fruit of the Spirit is the ultimate mark of a wholesome child of the King—love, joy, peace, patience, kindness, goodness, faithfulness, gentleness, and self-control (Galatians 5).

A healthy member of the second incarnation glorifies God by revealing the universals of God's character through the particulars of his everyday life. Billboards, tracts, movies, and books are all fine, but not as substitutes for a living epistle who makes love a way of life. Jesus said, "All men will know that you are my disciples if you love one another" (John 13:35). Love bound by holiness is the ultimate expression of God's presence in human experience.

In a nutshell, the product of the church's corporate life and ministry must be a person who has been liberated to love. In 1 Timothy 1:5, Paul tells Timothy that the ultimate aim of his ministry is love. When that love is felt, the message is heard. But none of us are lovers by nature. We are self-centered and self-seeking. In large measure we are "unbelieving believers." Our lives still contain pockets of hardness, resistance, and unbelief. Although the new birth begins a transformation which climaxes in the Lord's presence, we all struggle with questionable motives, unwholesome desires, and self-centered actions and reactions.

THE PRODUCTS FOR HEALTH

The church, God's beauty parlor, is the transforming community which *should* move believers toward a life of concern and care for others. I say "should" because movement toward love does not take place automatically. Even sound preaching is no guarantee that the listeners are being conformed to Christ's life style of love. The dynamics of the local body may actually have greater influence for change than the Sunday morning sermon. (I say this having been a pastor of a large church for seven years.) The church described in Acts 2 was a vital, dynamic fellowship that had great impact on its world. Christ loved it and it became beautiful. Locked away in Luke's description of this church are some critical qualities of a healthy, balanced believer. Here the text reveals that the *Holy Spirit uses believers with four distinguishing characteristics to build strong bodies.*

Learning That Lives

First, the believers "devoted themselves to the apostles' teaching" (Acts 2:42). Our church member must be a learning person… one who *continues* in the apostles' doctrine. When we cease to learn we cease to live. Many have died at age twenty and will be buried at seventy-five. The Word is our lamp and light. Scripture records that faith comes by hearing and hearing by the Word of God. Its truth must be hidden in our hearts (not in our frontal lobes) and practiced in our lives. It has been well stated that to know and not to do is not to know at all. Many pastors perceive the central purpose of their church as that of a Bible institute where facts are transmitted from one notebook to another. Doctrine becomes everything, as though understanding doctrine were an end unto itself. Unfortunately, a diet of doctrine alone will produce soul-sick people suffering from spiritual malnutrition. Usually their heads are full but their hearts are empty.

> Far too many people have used the Bible like a medical student uses a cadaver. They examine it, dissect it, perform surgery on it, familiarize themselves with it, and learn its distinctive qualities. But as that future doctor cannot give life to that dead piece of humanity, so these people never get the Word alive in their life. They somehow fail to remember that the people who hated Jesus most were biblical scholars and had Scriptures over their door posts, strapped to their bodies, and quoted chapters of it when their narrow-minded interpretation supported their warped views.[5]

Such churches can become like a baker who eats his own bread while a starving world gazes longingly through the bakery window.

Fellowship That Functions

The second characteristic of the Acts 2 Christian is that he *was involved in fellowship (koinonia).* "They devoted themselves to the apostles' teaching and to the fellowship" (Acts 2:42). This was not coffee and doughnuts between services. While *koinonia* involves the horizontal dimension (people to people), it is not fully understood unless it is linked with the vertical (individual to God). *Koinonia* involves both the church abiding in the vine for fruitfulness and the body being "joined and knit together" so that it can build itself up in love.

It is the fellowship of the Spirit which gives the dynamic, living, healing quality to the fellowship of the believers. In 2 Corinthians 13:14 Paul prays that "the fellowship of the Holy Spirit" may be with the believers in Corinth (cf. Philippians 2:1). Consequently, genuine fellowship cannot be duplicated outside the church. It is an atmosphere, an environment, and a set of attitudes and actions that grow and develop as Spirit-controlled believers meet and share their lives and giftedness together. It occurs when believers are together *under the direction of the Holy Spirit,* in an atmosphere conducive to the Spirit's empowering the body's gifts to change lives.

The Acts 2 Christian was a fellowshiping person. When he hurt he didn't bite a bullet and ride off into the sunset alone. He learned that the fellowship of believers was his source of strength, encouragement, rebuke, and motivation—the key to his growth. Fellowship takes place when pastoral leaders are faithful stewards of the gifts of the *entire body.* Most churches have one (or more) official pastor, and sometimes hundreds of "pastors on ice" who are never encouraged to minister because they lack proper training and certification.

The healthy believer grows because he has vital contact with the gifts of the *entire* body, not just the pastor on Sunday morning. It is sometimes difficult to recognize and appreciate that although many in a congregation have no formal training, some often know the Lord more intimately than the pastor. Others have valuable personal experiences the pastor lacks. Some have gifts the pastor doesn't have and these gifts need to be exercised if the church is to be balanced.

True fellowship and the free exercise of gifts are inseparable companions. A church can't have one without the other. All church programs should be evaluated in the light of their contribution to the free flow of the body's gifts. If the believer's sole exposure to the body is a one-way monologue on Sunday morning, chances are he does not experience the body as a healing communion.

The beauty-building body is always a body in which the believer is free to function properly. When the whole body functions under the Spirit's leadership, the believer experiences fellowship and the unbeliever sees beauty. The "one anothers" of the New Testament give us a helpful portrait of the kinds of actions that characterize the unique, divinely enabled fellowship of believers. Imagine the impact upon nonbelievers who observe believers relating to each other in this way. They will ask us the reason for the hope that is in us.

Reference	Statement
Romans 12:10	Be devoted to one another Give preference to one another
Romans 12:16	Be of same mind toward one another
Romans 13:8	Love one another
Romans 14:13	Let us not judge one another
Romans 14:19	Pursue the things that make for the building up of one another
Romans 15:5	Be of the same mind with one another
Romans 15:7	Accept one another
Romans 15:14	Admonish one another
1 Corinthians 12:25	Care for one another
Galatians 5:13	Serve one another
Galatians 6:2	Bear one another's burdens
Ephesians 4:1-2	Show forbearance to one another
Ephesians 4:32	Be kind to one another
Ephesians 5:18-21	Speak to one another in psalms and hymns and spiritual songs Be subject to one another
Colossians 3:9	Lie not to one another
Colossians 3:12-13	Bear with one another Forgive each other
Colossians 3:16	Teach and admonish one another

1 Thessalonians 3:12	Increase and abound in love for one another
1 Thessalonians 4:18	Comfort one another
Hebrews 3:13	Encourage one another
Hebrews 10:23-25	Stimulate one another to love and good works
James 4:11	Do not speak against one another
James 5:9	Do not complain against one another
James 5:16	Confess your sins to one another Pray for one another
1 Peter 1:22	Love one another
1 Peter 4:9	Be hospitable to one another
1 Peter 5:5	Clothe yourselves with humility toward one another
1 Peter 5:14	Greet one another with a kiss of love
1 John 3:11	Love one another
1 John 3:23	Love one another
1 John 4:7	Love one another
1 John 4:11	Love one another
1 John 4:12	Love one another
2 John 5	Love one another

I can visualize Jesus Christ graphically fulfilling this list of "body functions." We are called to do the same! Christ does his work of evangelism through not only our teaching but also our fellowship. Fellowship is the context in which the contagion of the good news is caught. Its significance for evangelism is not widely perceived. In the early church, however, it probably attracted as many to the Savior as the apostolic preaching. "Effective communication of the gospel begins with a demonstration of its relevance."[6] Incidentally, some of the best fellowship springs from the overflow of successful, consistent evangelism.

What kind of a person do we want to deploy into the world? Someone who is devoting himself to the apostles' teaching and to the fellowship.

Worship That Witnesses

Acts 2 goes on to describe a balanced believer as one who *worships:* "They devoted themselves...to the breaking of bread and to prayer...praising God" (2:42,47). Worship is *acknowledging the person and presence of God and responding with praise, thanksgiving, and obedience.* What kind of a person is the worshiping Christian? The worshiping Christian is not a worrying Christian. God's presence makes worship an antidote to worry. Though surrounded by enemies, one who worships can sit down to a leisurely meal because *God* prepares "a table before me in the presence of my enemies" (Psalm 23:5). The worshiping Christian affirms the presence of God's rod and staff when the battle rages in the midst of enemy territory.

Our Acts 2 Christian lived in a bloody, ruthless age. His life was continually in danger because of the Roman emperors' insane hatred of Christians. Martyrdom was common. The ranks of the local fellowship were thinned regularly by Rome's murderers. Yet the church grew, thrived, and worshiped triumphantly, proclaiming in word and deed the Lord's presence among them. The song says it so well, "Have you seen Jesus My Lord? He's here in plain view." The early church made him visible, and the results are history.

One of the side benefits of genuine worship is what I call attitude formation and maintenance. The worshiping person is a positive person because he has a certain, solid hope regardless of life's circumstances. He is a victor, a participant in God's sovereign, unalterable purposes. As he grows in his understanding of doctrine, his worship deepens and his attitudes change. As difficulty increases or discouragement creeps in, worship keeps his perspective focused on God.

What actions and attitudes characterize a worshiper? How does one worship? Worship is sensing Christ's presence, lifting him up, exalting him, responding to him, with hearts filled with praise and thanksgiving, ready to respond in obedience. Again, worship is an attitude that can be communicated. And our Christian "product" must be exposed to genuine worship if he is to be a dynamic, credible ambassador of Jesus Christ. Filled to overflowing with praise and gratitude for his God, *a worshiper witnesses by the simple spillage of the bounty of his heart.*

Instead of worshiping, many church leaders schedule "worship services." They hope that architecture, robes, pipe organs, and stained-glass voices will create an emotional tremor that will crack the spiritual ice. Too often God gets lost among the props. When we worship, we move from contemplation of God to communion with him. Unless we sense and respond to the Person of God, genuine worship does not take place.

A body of believers plays an important role in communicating worship. Worship has both a *context* and *content.* It can take place anywhere (context), but factual information about the person and work of God (content) comes largely (though not exclusively) from two sources: the written Word and "living epistles." This brings us back to the first two factors of teaching and fellowship. To worship effectively, then, I need exposure to God's Word and to God's people.

Healthy worship is the product of healthy teaching and healthy fellowship. Healthy teaching systematically works through the whole counsel of God. As the pastor exposes his people to God's attributes and character, his marvelous plan of salvation, his actions in history, and his promises for present day living, the believer is prepared to respond in worship. Provision for fellowship allows believers to identify the presence and work of God in their present experience. Consequently, we rejoice together because of who he is and the great things he has done. We praise him as we openly share his work on our behalf. We worship as evidence of his continued faithfulness builds to a crescendo and we acknowledge his Person and presence. When we gather on Sunday morning, our worship can be genuine because our fellowship with him and his children has been genuine throughout the week.

Serving That Sacrifices

Finally, the Spirit of God builds healthy bodies by using believers who are ready for service. "Selling their possessions and goods, they gave to anyone as he had need....And the Lord added to their number daily" (Acts 2:45,47). Mark it well, friend, the non-Christian *saw beauty*. They saw uncommon responses and experienced unusual care and concern. Because of believers' Christ-like attitudes and their sacrificial love, they enjoyed the favor of *all* the people, and God *added to their number daily*. They were candidates for the blessing of God! God was delighted to put new babies in this incubator.

A caring, loving will to serve is basic to evangelism because it provides credibility for the message of the gospel. The church community that reaches out to serve, to give, to sacrifice, and to care will be effective in evangelism.

What kind of person do we want to deploy into the world? A learning, fellowshiping, worshiping, serving person. Why do Christians not get involved in serving? Maybe it's because their learning is unrelated to life, their fellowship is sterile, and their worship is contrived. A well-taught, fellowshiping, worshiping person serves automatically. Evangelism for him is not a Tuesday night event; he is on duty twenty-four hours a day. His whole life is a living and willing sacrifice, a sweet savor to God and men. He offers himself as a living sacrifice knowing that it is no longer he but Christ who dwells in him, who reaches out to a needy world.

Evangelism is what Christ does through the preaching, fellowship, worship, and service of his bride. Realizing this great fact, the believer presents himself to be an instrument for noble purposes. The qualities of Christ will be built into his life if they are present and honored in the circle of his associations. Because his personality is a product of his relationships, it is imperative that we now consider the nature of the church, his transforming community.

Notes

1. James Engel, *Contemporary Christian Communications* (Nashville: Thomas Nelson Publishers, 1979), 30.

2. Ibid., 31.

3 . C. B . Hogue, *Love Leaves No Choice* (Waco, Tex.: Word Books, 1976), 31-32.

4. Engel, *Christian Communications,* 238.

5. Bailey E. Smith, *Real Evangelism* (Nashville: Broadman Press, 1978), 59.

6. George Hunter III, *The Contagious Congregation* (Nashville: Abingdon Press, 1979), 39.

CHAPTER 6

Evangelism and the Church Body

*H*umpty Dumpty was pushed." The street philosopher whose insight graced the side of a building captured a truth we all identify with. Brokenness is a deep-seated feeling which haunts all of us at one time or another. We are broken people in a broken world. We await the arrival of the king's men to reassemble us. Despite their best efforts, we still feel like last year's model. This sensed inadequacy often proves to be a crippling liability if we are not members of a healthy, growing church family.

Fortunately God's mission for us in this world does not wait until the reassembly process is completed. He sends us out into the world as salt and light even as he seasons the salt and trims the wick. Healthy believers recognize the growth process as a natural one and welcome each other as church members who are *all* (pastor and board members, too) under construction.

THE PURPOSES OF A HEALTHY CHURCH

If the person we deploy into the world is going to be effective as salt and light, then he must be the product of a church which takes beauty seriously. In chapter 5 we discussed the kind of person this should be. The next logical question is *"What kind of church makes possible that kind of person?"*

> Question One: What kind of person do we want to deploy into the world?
>
> Question Two: What kind of church makes possible that kind of person?

This second question is critical because *we become like the people we associate with.* Building on the qualities of the "Acts 2 Christian" (chapter 5) we can project the necessary functions of a healthy church that produces healthy church members. The healthy believer had four qualities: he was a learning, fellowshiping, worshiping, serving person. A balanced diet of these elements produces a wholesome, winsome individual who becomes a candidate for effective witness. Let's take each of these four qualities and relate them to a healthy local church.

To be a learning person who "continues in the apostles' teaching," one's church must be a *learning center.* To be a "fellowshiping person" fully exposed to the giftedness of the body, his church must be a *healing communion.* To be a worshiping person, his church must be a *responding community.* To be significantly involved in service, the church must be a *deploying agency.*

Individual	Church
Learning	Learning Center
Fellowshiping	Healing Communion
Worshiping	Responding Community
Serving	Deploying Agency

A Learning Center

We cannot minimize the pastor's role in enabling the church to be an effective learning center. He serves as both an educator and a model. Both dimensions of his ministry are crucial. Good, systematic biblical teaching programs the mind and heart of the individual and challenges him to respond in obedience to God. Under such teaching, divine boundaries are established, God's principles of life are set forth, and his person and work are clearly portrayed. The effective pastor not only presents the concepts and precepts of Scripture, but he relates them to everyday concerns. The possibility of wholesome, positive Christian living is continually reinforced. In his presentation of biblical truth, he paints a portrait of what the individual can *become* and *do.* Change can come because of the divine provision available to each believer. Napoleon was right when he said, "A man becomes the man of his uniform." The effective pastor continually works at visualizing new choices and possibilities for his people as he models these qualities in his own life.

Believing that it is a sin to bore people with God's Word, the effective pastor works diligently to present truth with impact. His goal is not to teach the Bible (it doesn't need to be taught anything). His purpose is to teach *people* —real, live, breathing, hurting people—the Bible.

The obedient pastor is to produce the same climate for growth that God produces for his children. Ephesians 3:17 says that God has rooted and grounded us in the soil of his love, and it is from this soil that we are to draw our nourishment and strength. As members of one another, we too must function together in love if the body is to become a healing communion. It is the effective preaching of the Word which provides the context for genuine fellowship.

The focus of such teaching should be edification, not evangelism. As a general rule, the "church gathered" comes together to be built up in the faith; the "church scattered" is to be involved in evangelism. An altar call every Sunday should be carefully rethought. It is, like the Sunday school, of recent origin, a unique development of American Protestantism.

> It has no clear precedent in the traditional worship of the Reformation, or even in the spiritual exercises in the Protestant revival movements in the seventeenth or early eighteenth centuries. Neither the Puritans, the Pietists, nor the Methodists, all of whom figured so prominently in setting the pattern for spiritual life of early America, had an intrinsic notion of 'the altar call' in their public order of worship. [1]

Whatever else could be said, the altar call should be used wisely and with integrity.

A Healing Communion

Fellowship reinforces the truth taught and links it with personal experience for added impact. As an educator, the pastor must understand and acknowledge the educational implications of fellowship. The believer challenged by the preached Word on Sunday morning can find counsel and support for implementation of the truth if vital fellowship is a regular part of the church life. The reservoir of truth, filled on Sunday morning, must become a river of blessing during the week. It is in the context of fellowship that the giftedness of the entire body is most capable of functioning. The father struggling with the discipline of his children may discover the *need* for a biblical approach on Sunday morning and get *specifics* from other members during the week as he shares his concerns with them. Getting these specifics requires exposure to the counsel and concern (giftedness) of others. And there is no substitute for the real life, down-to-earth sharing of truth as it is experienced in everyday living.

At the church where I served as pastor, we had dozens of men's groups meeting weekly. Much healing took place as these men shared 1) the *Word* and *prayer,* 2) their *schedules,* and 3) their *relationships.* Meeting in supportive groups of three or four, they became catalysts to one another's spiritual growth as they held each other accountable. Important schedule items (appointments, decisions) were shared as prayer requests. Relationship concerns were communicated regularly. It was not unusual to set aside ten to fifteen minutes for consideration of our wives' and families' needs. Having written down needs in each area, the men would identify the two or three most urgent ones and describe their plans to meet them that week. Held accountable to follow through, the men did so, and growth was the happy result.

Accountability is an important key to growth. It's the key to Weight-Watchers. Their scales, diets, and exercises are probably not superior to any other weight loss clinic. What gets the weight off are their regular group sessions, which include a weigh in.

Accountability is so often missing. Where it is present, growth inevitably follows. Wives would say to me, "Joe, I don't know what's going on in those groups, but keep it up!" Simply stated, the men were learning how to love each other, and the skills are transferable! It is doubtful such learning could take place Sunday morning no matter how eloquent the pastor. Home Bible studies provide another significant context for the experience of vital fellowship. In such groups, needs can be shared, experiences communicated, and gifts exercised in such a way that real growth and healing take place.

Unfortunately, the very dynamics which cause growth are killed by growth. In the beginning stages everyone knows everyone and each family contributes to the ongoing ministry of the fellowship. Everyone feels needed and important. But numerical growth tends to depersonalize relationships and dilute fellowship. This leaves the growing church with the task of decentralization, a function accomplished by encouraging and providing for vital fellowship in a small group setting. Believers need to meet together as a mighty army in celebration and worship, but they also need to be a part of a small band where supportive fellowship can be a reality. Only then is the church freed to be a healing communion.

The responsible church leader must examine the programming of his church in light of his people's need for fellowship. In many cases, the church has lost all sight of body function and has made the forms (programs) sacred. Success is often measured by whether a particular program has grown numerically, rather than on its contribution to the free flow of the giftedness of the body. How can we say we are committed to strengthening the family, for example, when our church programs often take parents away from time with their children? Pastors often cannot believe it when I tell them I was at home six nights a week as pastor of a very large church. A biblical philosophy of ministry makes such an option a possibility.

A Responding Community

Sound teaching and healthy fellowship set the stage for worship. The healthy church is a *responding community* in which God "inhabits the praise of his people." The joy of relationship leads the family to the triumphal celebration and worship of their heavenly Father. Growing in love with him, captivated by his grace, his people respond in obedience and service. When the spiritual life of a congregation is weak, it is most evident at the level of worship. In a positive sense, the vitality of the church is best indicated by the nature of its worship. Programs, budgets, facilities, and numbers can be deceiving. God is seeking those who will worship him in spirit and truth.

Such worship leads to commitment and service. "Worship expresses itself in witness; witness fulfills itself in worship. The unifying theme is the glory of God and of His Christ, and there is a great need for this to be the Supreme incentive of our modern evangelism."[2] Worship which does not produce witness is hypocrisy. "Worship that is pleasing to God will inevitably send us out to bear witness of the Name we have sought to honor."[3]

A Deploying Agency

Motivated by sound teaching, encouraged and equipped by the body, God's children lift up their eyes unto the fields ripe for harvest. The vision for service is constantly cultivated by a teaching, fellowshiping, and worshiping family. A healthy fellowship, undergirded by good teaching and joyful worship, produces committed disciples and makes for a beautiful bride.

This process of *edification* is dependent upon the *proper functioning* of each individual part of the body and ultimately upon Christ himself. Christ, the head of the body, orchestrates the functioning of each part as it uses its special gift for the betterment of the body. He nourishes his bride by leading her into growth-producing teaching, fellowship, and worship.

The long-term result is holy character and blameless conduct. These qualities, engraved by Christ's Spirit, make Christians living epistles read by all men. It is his desire that we become suitable reading material. Christ works directly through the church's *message (kerygma)*, its *fellowship (koinonia),* and its *worship* and *service (diakonia)* to draw men to himself.[4] The drama of redemption as it is taught, lived, and experienced gives evangelism its impact. Evangelism is not something we do for Christ; it is something he does through us.

Christ

Nourishes

through
Teaching
Fellowship
Worship

Cherishes

Church
(bride)

increasingly
Holy
Character

increasingly
Blameless
Conduct

Beautiful Living Epistles
who serve by

Loving one another
Bearing one another's
burdens
Encouraging one
another
Stimulating one
another to love
and good works

Accepting one another
Forgiving one another
Being kind to one
another
Comforting one another
Bearing with one another

The World
observes and responds as it
1. Hears the Teachings (krygma)
2. Observes the Fellowship (koinonia)
3. Experiences the Love (diakonia)

Edification (Beautifying the Bride)

Evangelism (Displaying the Bride)

The critical question is, "What are nonbelievers reading?" Is the message music to their ears? Arnold Toynbee once stated that "most people have not rejected Christianity but a caricature." How tragic that many have rejected Christ because the bride was not very Christlike. Like real people, the body of Christ has its diseases which tend to turn away rather than attract.

TO BE AVOIDED LIKE THE PLAGUE

The New Testament reveals four leavens or evil influences the body should avoid. They are evangelism killers. Their presence in the body is ugly and contaminates the reputation of the bride. To produce the kind of church which deploys beautiful people into a lost world, these leavens must be eliminated.

Four Marks of Ugliness
Enemies of Effective Evangelism

- Hypocrisy   (Matthew 16)
- Rationalism   (Matthew 16)
- Impurity   (1 Corinthians 5)
- Legalism   (Galatians 5)

These diseases eliminate effective service, destroy worship, distort fellowship, and cripple evangelism. They produce crippled, inconsistent, hypocritical "living epistles...read of all men."

The Spreading of Hypocrisy

In Matthew 16:6-12 our Lord warns his disciples about the influence of the Pharisees and Sadducees on the life and fellowship of the church. This leaven of the Pharisees is *religious externalism* or *hypocrisy*. When this disease prevails, church members get caught up in ritual without reality, motion without meaning.

Pharisees were "keepers of the old wineskins." They were upset with Christ because he didn't go along with the games Pharisees play. Christ's followers dismayed them by eating with dirty hands and picking grain on the Sabbath. The Pharisees would have loved to enroll Christ and his disciples in a finishing school where they would learn how to launder their lives, bleaching out any evidence of contact with publicans and sinners. The Pharisees were quick to establish spiritual pecking orders based on performance rather than character. As such, they produced tremendous pressure upon their contemporaries to conform to cultural standards they had established, most of which were not biblical. I hope some of the parallels are obvious.

Paul told Timothy that love, the ultimate aim of ministry, is possible when men are freed from hypocrisy: "The goal of this command is love, which comes from a pure heart and a good conscience and a sincere faith" (1 Timothy 1:5). The term *sincere* is actually the word *hypocrite* with the Greek letter *alpha* in front of it. It could be translated "unhypocritical." Note it carefully, friend: Love, the ultimate expression of God's presence, springs from a pure heart, a clear conscience, and a *life free of hypocrisy.*

Man's heart and conscience are part of his inner being and are invisible and unknowable to others. All we can observe is an individual's walk, his reaction to people and events, and his life style. Man's life style is like the tip of the iceberg; the rest is out of sight. God, the source of love, seeks human channels through whom he can express his love. We are not only messages to be read but instruments to be used. But God's love is *contaminated by an impure heart, confined by a guilty conscience,* and *counterfeited by a phony life style.*

If the leaven of hypocrisy is to be avoided, the church fellowship must adopt the principle that *maturity is always a return to reality* about God, oneself, and others. The maturing person wants to grow and recognizes his need for the input of other members of the body. We've all heard the unbeliever who doubts the sincerity of the local church because of hypocritical church members. We fight embarrassment and shame as he recounts the actions of unethical church leaders and reminds us of immorality in the choir loft, not to mention its inroads into the pastoral study.

To leave hypocrisy behind and grow toward authenticity, we need to develop an openness to *feedback* and *self-disclosure.* Feedback from others provides us with insight into areas of needed growth and development. The Bible says "As iron sharpens iron, so one man sharpens another" (Proverbs 27:17). If the local church which shapes the lives of those it deploys into the world is going to be a healthy, authentic, redemptive community, feedback among believers must be encouraged. Many have isolated themselves from the giftedness of the body by not being open to feedback. To grow, I must encourage believers to "speak the truth in love"…to me. They will not do it unless I encourage and welcome it.

Pride is probably the biggest enemy of authenticity. We fear losing the respect of our peers if we disclose that we are less than perfect and "standing in the need of prayer." But to have deep hurts, blind spots, and areas of inadequacy is not abnormal. It is abnormal—it is a counterfeit existence—when we attempt to cover inadequacy and refuse to deal with areas we need help in. A counterfeit is something that purports to be genuine but isn't. Counterfeits are accepted and respected until their inauthenticity is discovered. Then their credibility is lost, and their beauty turns to ugliness. Some therefore conclude that any disclosure of imperfection moves one into the camp of the hypocrites. Not so. Pretending to be perfect, pretending to be adequate, is hypocritical. Besides, self-disclosure should also be very positive. We need to be able to share our dreams, longings, and desires with a close friend who can give us encouragement, insight, and direction. Acknowledgment of our dependency and inadequacy can be a beautiful and encouraging act. Often the greatest gift we can share is the gift of our need.

If our model Christian deployed into the world is to be good news, he must be authentic, living *openly and communicating freely from the present stage of his pilgrimage toward wholeness.* He will have impact if he is part of a church fellowship committed to purity, integrity, and sincerity.

The Spreading of Unbelief

The Sadducees were antisupernaturalists. They didn't believe in the resurrection or in angelic beings. They treated the universe as a closed system subject only to natural forces. As an approach to life, rationalism limits human accomplishment to human ability. The rationalist has lost his vision of the sovereignty and providence of God and as a result is incapable of dreaming God-sized goals. Such a philosophy siphons away the divine dimensions of life and reduces Christianity to nothing but a glorified humanism.

Where there is no Spirit-given vision, there can be no effective evangelism. Believers must have their mental vision purged of all temporal, selfish, and limiting concerns. The biblical principle is vision-oriented evangelism. Only a Spirit-inspired vision of both man's lostness and God's available power can lift evangelism from an occasionally scheduled project to a total life style.

Men of vision live so all the time. The leaven of the Sadducees destroys vision. It is the epitome of unbelief. Churches afflicted with this disease are constantly checking their spiritual pulses and declaring, "It's useless, it cannot be done." Faith in God's provision is noticeably absent. Skepticism, pessimism, and apathy are apparent. The healthy church needs modern giant killers like David and Caleb who are "foolish" enough to believe God!

Many streams of thought feed the rationalistic channel, such as, "It's already been tried," or "It's too risky and will be embarrassing if it doesn't work." An unwillingness to depart from treasured traditions and forms stunts a faith that would reach out in contemporary fashion. And a rationalization of failures or inadequacies as "the way God would have it" can build a formidable foundation of rationalism in the minds of those who should believe in the God of miracles.

One subtle form of antisupernaturalism often grows out of a perverted, unbalanced view of God's sovereignty. Some pastors and leaders excuse the lack of supernatural, God-empowered growth and vitality by claiming that God must have willed it. To some it is folly to dream, to reach, to stretch, to plan, to believe and to act accordingly. A passive, ho-hum, wait-and-see attitude is not unusual. *But faith* is what pleases God. Not to take the promises of God out of mothballs and by faith apply them to the challenges of life is the ultimate mark of a Sadducee. Our Lord warned us to avoid such evil teaching.

My friendship through the years with Bill Bright, the founder and director of Campus Crusade for Christ, has been an important lesson in faith. Here is a man who believes God, takes his purposes seriously, and acts accordingly. I never go away from his presence without being challenged to believe God in a bigger way. May his tribe increase! The writer to the Hebrews reminds us that without faith it is not possible to please God (11:6). Our Acts 2 Christian needs to be surrounded by men and women of faith and vision.

The Spreading of Impurity

Paul introduces a third deadly leaven in 1 Corinthians 5, the leaven of impurity: "Don't you know that a little yeast [impurity] works through the whole batch of dough? Get rid of the old yeast that you may be a new batch without yeast—as you really are" (5:6-7). The proverbial expression, "One bad apple spoils the whole barrel," is true. Impurity spreads in a similar manner if it is not checked. All that is coarse, crude, and carnal must be avoided if a church is to be a candidate for God's blessing.

> It is God's will that you should be sanctified: that you should avoid sexual immorality; that each of you should learn to control his own body in a way that is holy and honorable...For God did not call us to be impure, but to live a holy life (1 Thessalonians 4:3-4, 7).

Love springs from a pure heart. No clever arrangement of rotten eggs will make a good omelet.

To make purity a reality, we must bring every thought into captivity to Christ so that he can fill our minds with "whatever is pure." It is imperative, then, to avoid contamination especially in our thought life. This fact often leads to misunderstanding when it comes to evangelism. At a pastor's conference I once was cornered by a pastor who was upset because I stressed the need to make friends with non-Christian neighbors. He insisted that the Bible taught that we were to love our enemies but not to be friends with them. The disagreement boiled down to a misunderstanding of the doctrine of separation. Separation is not isolation. It is living a distinctive, pure life in the midst of an impure world. It is being salt and light in the midst of darkness and death. It is being a living epistle available for others to read. There is no impact without contact, and contact can be risky. Our Lord avoided contamination, yet was accused of being a drunkard, a friend of publicans and sinners. He maintained purity in the midst of impurity.

The healthy church must deal immediately and directly with the disease of impurity. To allow impurity to function like yeast is to commit ecclesiastical suicide. It is from impurity *within* the body of Christ that the believer is to separate himself.

> I have written you in my letter not to associate with sexually immoral people—not at all meaning the people of this world who are immoral, or the greedy and swindlers, or idolaters. In that case you would have to leave this world. But now I *am writing you that you must not associate with anyone who calls himself a brother* but is sexually immoral or greedy, an idolater or a slanderer, a drunkard or a swindler. With such a man do not even eat (1 Corinthians 5:9-11).

Impurity within the body destroys the bride's beauty and discredits Christ, the bridegroom. Paul's instruction about such impurity is clear: "Clean out the old leaven." Healthy church discipline is a vital part of maintaining the testimony of the local church. It serves notice to the community that although the church consists of imperfect people moving toward wholeness, impurity is not acceptable as a way of life. Difficult as church discipline is, it can be a positive force for evangelism in that it declares to the community that the church intends, by God's grace, *to practice what it preaches.* Our Acts 2 Christian needs to be surrounded by people committed to purity.

The Spreading of Legalism

We are all legalists by nature. The church at Galatia fell into the trap of legalism, and Paul had to write to correct this dangerous error. Reminding them of their freedom in Christ he asked them, "You were running a good race; who cut in on you and kept you from obeying the truth?" Legalism is an ethical system which measures spirituality by one's compliance with an arbitrary set of rules. The legalist likes to think he has avoided the problem of worldliness. Holiness to him is a world-denying withdrawal, a radical otherworldliness. Such a definition ignores Paul's comments in Colossians 2:16, 20-22.

> Therefore do not let anyone judge you by what you eat or
> drink, or with regard to a religious festival, a New Moon cel-
> ebration or a Sabbath day....Since you died with Christ to
> the basic principles of this world, why, as though you still
> belonged to it, do you submit to its rules: "Do not handle!
> Do not taste! Do not touch!"? These are all destined to perish
> with use, because they are based on human commands and
> teachings.

Worldliness, according to Paul, is a legalistic preoccupation
with eating and drinking and Sabbath keeping; it is "a legalistic
preoccupation with conformity to a man-made code of don'ts."[5]
The following quote is a classic illustration of legalistic preoccupation: "We preach against every form of worldliness including
television, newspapers, smoking, drinking, worldly amusements,
improper dress, and even against coffee, tea, Coca-Cola, and
overeating."[6]

In his attempt to avoid worldliness, the legalist is snared in its
very trap. The rules of the legalist are usually cultural rather than
biblical. Legalism has killed the evangelistic impact of countless
churches because legalism is *pure, unadulterated ugliness.* Not only
is it ugly, it fails in its purpose.

> Our young people know how long to wear their hair, how
> short their skirts should be, that it is wrong to go to the
> movies; and all the while they are taking drugs and trying to
> decide about premarital sex. We are often as irrelevant with
> our set of rules as the oral traditions of the Jews which had a
> rule for each day."[7]

It is so much easier to draw up lists and bury ourselves
behind self-imposed laws than to come to grips with our freedom
in Christ. Like a frontal lobotomy, legalism severs the nerve of life
and vitality and leaves its victims breathing but not beautiful. It is
a subtle sin, but sin nevertheless.

A legalist suffers from the following symptoms. He is a great
fence builder with the compulsive need to label and categorize
people, places, and things. Like some health food fanatics, he
knows not only what is wrong for him, but also for everyone else.
He tends to act as a self-appointed judge and jury, and assumes
the role of joy-robber whose prey is the body of Christ. A person

with this mental framework is ineffective in reaching the lost, having constructed barriers based on unbiblical presuppositions about separation. Unlike Paul who "became all things to all men," the legalist is rigid, inflexible, and unbending.

If the church is going to take beauty seriously, it must face ugliness with integrity. To be beautiful, we need to associate with beautiful people. An old adage says that "poor people need to take rich people out to dinner and listen because success leaves clues." Pick out someone in your church who has that special "radiance" and spend some time together. Ask yourself what it is that makes your friend distinctive and attractive. If some of your friends are suffering from a severe case of hardening of the attitudes, perhaps you can be God's instrument to nudge them toward a more balanced, wholesome, authentic life style.

Your association with a loving, caring, supportive family is the key to your personal beauty and a major factor in your evangelistic effectiveness. Work hard at eliminating the leavens of hypocrisy, rationalism, impurity, and legalism.

DEVELOP DIVINE SIGNPOSTS

"Eliminate the negative, accentuate the positive" isn't bad advice. Besides eliminating diseases, what positive influences should the church be showing and spreading from the overflow of its gathered life? The New Testament describes four corporate qualities which let the nonbeliever know that God is revealing himself in this world. These are *love, unity, good works,* and *hope.* Each of these qualities is singled out for its evangelistic impact. When they are observed and felt by the non-Christian, something uniquely divine is communicated. These qualities serve as divine signposts for the nonbeliever, signposts that lead him toward the foot of the cross.

Divine Signposts
Love
Unity
Good Works
Hope

The Display of Love

Defining love is like mental housekeeping in a revolving door. Most of our descriptions are *lexical* in nature, like dictionary definitions: "Love is seeking the highest good of its object." Not bad, but not very helpful. Sometimes our definitions are *behavioral*. Love is washing dishes or cleaning the sink or scrubbing the tub. Not too romantic, but realistic and observable. Occasionally we use *experiential* definitions of love such as, "I feel loved when you listen, when you spend time with me, when you forgive me." Our Lord said, "All men will know that you are my disciples if you love one another" (John 13:35). Notice several important principles growing out of Christ's remarkable statement.

First, love is more than a warm glow somewhere inside. It is an observable, tangible phenomenon which takes place between people. When love acts it can be seen, felt, and experienced by others.

Second, love as seen, felt, and experienced is somehow linked with Christ in the mind of the nonbeliever. "All men will know that you are my disciples if you love..." A genuine love relationship focuses the nonbeliever's attention in the right direction. It probably is the key to changing the nonbeliever's attitude toward the gospel from a negative to a positive. When the Spirit of God writes the script, growing, loving relationships are the result. When the nonbeliever reads that script, he recognizes its divine authorship.

Third, love can be chosen or shunned by the believer—it is not a guaranteed attitude for one who has chosen Christ. "All men will know...*if* you love one another." Over and over the New Testament writers exhort, admonish, and warn believers about the necessity of love. The opposites of love are not very attractive. Our model Christian, deployed into the world, must be part of a loving, caring community if he is to be effective in evangelism. (We will discuss some practical means of expressing love in a later chapter.)

The Display of Unity

Unity is another divine signpost for our non-Christian friends. It, like love, focuses their attention in the right direction. God, as it were, surfaces and becomes visible when believers live together in unity. Paul's instructions in Ephesians 4:2-3 link love and unity together: "Be completely humble and gentle; be patient, bearing with one another in love. Make every effort to keep the unity of the Spirit through the bond of peace." A similar connection is found in our Lord's prayer for his bride: "May they be brought to complete unity to let the world know that you sent me and have loved them even as you have loved me" (John 17:23).

When a local assembly is characterized by unity, the world observes two important facts. First, the remarkable, distinctive quality of unity communicates to the world that God sent Christ. Genuine unity is such a rare commodity that when disciples of Christ have it, an observer concludes Christ is a man sent from God himself. Notice carefully that Christ prays for *unity*, not *uniformity*. Where there are great pressures for uniformity, we should be suspicious. Christians do not have to look, dress, think, and act alike. The church is not an assembly line producing only Fords. If a church has genuine unity, it isn't overly concerned with uniformity. Most of the pressures for uniformity focus around cultural rather than biblical issues, although many who push for uniformity *assume* they are biblical issues.

Unity attracts the blessing of God. "How good and pleasant it is," writes the psalmist, "when brothers live together in unity.… There the LORD bestows his blessing" (Psalm 133). Humility is the foundation of unity. Folks can most effectively live out their faith corporately in a posture of humility and unity. God always resists the proud, but gives grace to the humble.

Unity is the highest form of evangelism. God pours out his blessing where it is present. (For a full development of the necessity and power of unity, see my book *Prayer Summits: Seeking God's Agenda for Your Community*.) At the heart of every successful ministry is a core of leaders who love each other and dwell together in unity. The converse is also true.

Satan is the great enemy of unity. He divided the angelic ranks, split the first family, split the monarchy of Israel, and has split the church wide open. Unity is the result of all believers being joined to Christ and joined to one another. We are not commanded to make unity but to maintain it, not simply in individual churches but in the broader family of faith.

Legalism is also an enemy of unity because it assumes unity means uniformity. When "unity" is obtained in a legalistic community, its members usually become cult-like zombies, stripped of the individual sparkle of true Christian vitality. The corporate life style becomes bland and contrived. When the beauty of the Christ who refused to be bottled in old wineskins is replaced with Pharisaic legalism, evangelistic effectiveness is greatly impaired.

Biblical unity encourages a healthy diversity which is essential for beauty and authenticity. The creative genius of the Holy Spirit has endowed us with an amazing diversity of gifts, abilities, and cultural distinctives. Salvation does not destroy such diversities; rather it redeems and enhances them, bringing them under the Lordship of Christ.

Our model Christian needs to be part of a fellowship marked by unity. Church fights, family feuds, power plays, politicking, and manipulation do not attract men and women to Christ. Many "spiritual banty roosters" need to have their wings clipped!

The Display of Good Works

Believers are "created in Christ Jesus to do good works, which God prepared in advance for us to do" (Ephesians 2:10). Good works are also a powerful tool for evangelism. The helpful, supportive, encouraging, sacrificial actions of believers become significant signposts for the nonbeliever. "Live such good lives among the pagans that, though they accuse you of doing wrong, they may see your good deeds and glorify God on the day he visits us" (1 Peter 2:12). To say that they will see our good works presupposes activity. The Spirit-filled Christian is a busy person, actively engaged in the business of the King. Evangelism involves active, diligent effort.

The New Testament pattern of evangelism is a blend of proclamation and practical meeting of needs. The hungry were fed, the sick ministered to, the naked clothed, and the widows and fatherless cared for. The music of the believers' selfless actions became the platform for the words of the gospel. The world, observing this care, commented on their love for each other. Thousands of believers willingly marched into Alexandria, Egypt, during the plague and gave their lives to minister to the dying. Many sold themselves into slavery in the salt mines so they could minister to fellow believers held in bondage, never again to see the light of day. As the Roman persecutions grew in intensity, long lines of chained Christians were dragged to Rome for execution. Christians from local villages walked with them, ministering to their physical and spiritual needs. Their presence often turned these tragic, beastly marches into triumphal processions.

The bottom line is that you and I should excel at meeting needs through our good works. We are created by God for the purpose of *doing good works!* Cultivators specialize in good works, which are simply practical expressions of love. We know that faith without works is dead faith. Genuine faith produces a life style characterized by good works. Our love is to find practical, tangible expression through our actions. As we cultivate, the good news is translated into deeds. It is good news when a drunkard is loved out of his alcoholic hell. It is good news when an adulterous husband is restored to his wife and family. It is good news when Christians adopt the fatherless and care for the abandoned and hopeless. It is divine music when believers apply what they profess to the hurts and sorrows of mankind.

The Holy Spirit has gifted each of us with abilities which are channels for his love toward both the Christian and non-Christian communities. These abilities include spiritual gifts as well as special skills such as carpentry, plumbing, cooking, and gardening. God has used my gift of teaching as a vehicle for good works. I also know He has used my abilities with a hammer and saw to win some neighbors to Christ. My wife's cooking abilities have been the channel through which God's love has been felt by numerous non-Christian neighbors, many of whom have become believers. Some cultivate, others sow, and others reap.

A community of believers, freed by the Spirit to live beyond selfishness, becomes increasingly powerful to witness as it makes good works a way of life. The First Southern Baptist Church of Del City, Oklahoma, disturbed because of an X-rated theater near the church, purchased the theater and now uses it to show Christ-centered movies. On Sunday afternoons as many as six hundred children are exposed to the gospel through a free movie and Bible lesson. Our deployed Christian needs to be part of a church family known and respected for its good works.

The Display of Hope

"Always be prepared to give an answer to everyone who asks you to give the reason for the hope that you have" (1 Peter 3:15). Hope is another divine signpost which captures the attention of the nonbeliever living in this despair-filled world. Children of the King must not allow the world's pessimism to poison their heritage of hope. Christians and non-Christians share life's tragedies, sorrows, and hurts. But we do not "grieve like the rest of men, who have no hope" (1 Thessalonians 4:13). The nonbeliever who observes the Christian facing life's trials with hope and optimism is going to want to know what creates such a response. Peter says he will ask you the reason for your hope. Peter's underlying premise is that believers will have significant enough relationships with non-Christians that hope has a serious chance of being observed. Hope is most powerful when it is observed against the backdrop of seeming hopelessness. When the non-Christian is allowed to share in some of these experiences, the music of the gospel plays loud and clear.

But hope is not simply a response to difficult circumstances. It is also a permanent, settled attitude toward life. There is no room for an attitude of pessimism to rule in the life of God's children. The deployed Christian needs to surround himself with hope-filled, optimistic believers. The magnetic power of hope stands as an intriguing possibility for the searching nonbeliever. Could he, too, discover a reason to be filled with hope?

Love, unity, good works, and hope adorn the beautiful bride, calling attention to her divine lineage. These divine signposts contrast sharply with the diseases of hypocrisy, unbelief, impurity, and legalism which weaken an ailing church. But the signposts awaken the passerby to a healthy church that produces learning, fellowshiping, worshiping, serving members—God's medicine for a sick world. The healthy church members who fill healthy church bodies aren't in good shape by accident. They are led into a life style of health. By whom? We'll answer that question in the next chapter.

Notes

1. Robert E. Coleman, "The Origin of the Altar Call in American Methodism," *Asbury Seminarian* (Winter 1958): 19.

2. John R. Stott, *Our Guilty Silence* (Grand Rapids: Wm. B. Eerdmans Publishing Co., 1969), 27.

3. Ibid., 25.

4. George Hunter III, *The Contagious Congregation* (Nashville: Abingdon Press, 1979), 28.

5. Vernon Grounds, "Loving the World: Rightly or Wrongly," *Christianity Today,* 4 April 1980, 20.

6. Peter S. Ruckman, "More Baloney from BJU," *Bible Believers' Bulletin* , 3 July 1980, 1.

7. Thomas Dollar, *Baptist Bulletin,* February 1980, 1.

CHAPTER 7

Evangelism and the Church Leadership

For years I have respected the Weatherby name and tradition. The machined precision, quality materials, and excellent craftsmanship which go into a Weatherby rifle make it a thing of beauty. All the evidence I could accumulate from magazines and personal recommendations confirmed the excellence of the product. Weatherby has done its "pre-evangelism" well; its "music" is very good.

One day a young man named Ed Weatherby started attending the church I pastored. Imagine my pleasure when I discovered that he was part of the famed Weatherby family. The day he took me through the Weatherby plant I thought I'd died and gone to heaven. I met his father, Roy Weatherby, sat in his trophy-filled office, and talked enthusiastically about their famous products. There is something to be learned from the Weatherby tradition. With Weatherby's emphasis on *quality assurance* and *quality control*, the rifle sells itself. There is no better marketing than a satisfied customer!

If our local churches are to be beautiful, wholesome expressions of the bride of Christ, someone must devote himself to quality assurance and control. *Quality assurance* is concerned with defining quality and devising a strategy to produce it. *Quality control* is concerned with the maintenance of quality once it is assured. Quality is not an accident. The church that deploys into the community wholesome, winsome believers has leaders who take quality seriously.

This leads us to our third question about an evangelistically effective church: *What kind of leadership team makes possible that kind of church?* Let's review our previous questions.

> Question One: What kind of person do we want to deploy into the world?

> Question Two: What kind of church makes possible that kind of person?

> Question Three: What kind of leadership team makes possible that kind of church?

The first question attempts to define a *product* whose qualities assure maximum effectiveness. Since our model Christian is a product of the church he attends, the second question attempts to discuss a *process* that will assure a quality product. Our third question focuses on a prototype *pattern* or behavioral model that illustrates through example the way the body is to function—and then makes sure that quality pattern is produced.

LEADERSHIP: A QUICK LOOK AT THE WHOLE CHURCH

The leadership team is a microcosm of the body. It is the prototype, the mini-church for the rest of the congregation. Depending on church polity, the leaders are usually called elders or deacons. *The life style of leadership determines the life style of the body which in turn determines the life style of the one deployed into the world.* The behavioral model for the congregation is the leadership team.

Loving, caring, authentic Christian communities are not produced by church board members who sow discord and strife. The quality of relationships between board members is one of the most critical factors in the church's evangelistic impact. Wherever I go to speak at pastors conferences, I hear a recurring theme: The board can't get along; they're feuding, they're manipulating and seeking their own interests. It is not unusual to find board members in direct opposition to each other and the pastor.

When leaders lack unity, they poison the body and hinder evangelistic effectiveness. If the leaders are not characterized by love and support for each other, there is little chance for such qualities to be present in the corporate fellowship. Knowing that "precept begins but example accomplishes," leaders must strive to be worthy models to follow.

Remember our Lord's statement. When a pupil is fully taught, when a man is fully discipled, *he will be like* his teacher. Paraphrasing John 13:35 we could say that "the congregation will know for certain that their leaders are true disciples of Christ (and therefore worthy models to follow) if they have love for one another." Imagine the power and the impact for change if leaders related as Paul describes in 1 Corinthians 13 (I have substituted the word *leader* for *love* to help make the point):

> The leader is so patient and kind;
> He never boils with jealousy;
> He never boasts, is never puffed with pride;
> He does not act with rudeness or insist on his rights;
> He never gets provoked, never harbors evil thoughts;
> He is never glad when wrong is done,
> But always glad when truth prevails;
> He bears up under everything;
> He exercises faith in everything;
> He keeps up hope in everything.
>
> (Adapted from Williams translation of the New Testament)

THE NECESSITY OF MODELING BY LEADERSHIP

Peter underscores the necessity of modeling as he writes,

> I beg the elders among you, be shepherds of the flock of God that is among you, not as though you had to but of your own free will, not from the motives of personal profit but freely, and not as domineering over those in your charge *but proving yourselves models* for the flock to imitat (1 Peter 5:1b-3, Williams).

Peter's words deserve careful consideration. Sheep need shepherds who assume responsibility for the welfare of the flock. Furthermore, shepherds are not to minister because they have to but because they freely choose to care for others. The issue is not skill, gift, or experience, but rather desire. The leader must like people. As an undershepherd, he is to love the sheep as Christ the Great Shepherd does. The shepherd knows his sheep. He calls them by name and they follow him. The leader (shepherd) serves with no motive of personal profit or gain. Unfortunately, some go into the ministry to do good, and end up doing very well. The position is not to be sought as a status symbol or mark of prestige. It is an opportunity to serve others, committing oneself to their growth, recognition, and achievement.

The leader does not pull rank to accomplish his purposes. He leads by example. He is not to domineer or "lord it over" those in his charge. The business world's emphasis on *position power* is not an acceptable model for local church leadership. Our Lord taught this same truth in Luke 22 where he said, "The kings of the Gentiles lord it over them; and those who exercise authority over them call themselves Benefactors. *But you are not to be like that.* Instead, the greatest among you should be like the youngest, and the one who rules like the one who serves....But I am among you as one who serves" (22:25-26, 27b). This same Christ, the head of the church, loved her and *gave himself up for her* so that she could advance toward beauty and royalty (Ephesians 5:25-27).

This principle of imitation presupposes the existence of a distinctive, God-given life style. Detailed descriptions of the character qualities of the leader, our behavioral model, can be found in 1 Timothy 3 and Titus 1. These passages reveal the kind of leadership necessary to produce a beauty parlor that actually produces beauty. The rest of this chapter will discuss these important qualifications.

Finally, because the leader leads by example, he must live intentionally. It must be said of him that he "lived a purposeful, distinctive life among believers for their sake" (1 Thessalonians 1:5, Williams). Effective church leaders *choose* to live and relate to each other in specific, observable, and agreed upon ways. They schedule quality time together because quality relationships take time. Our church board met twice each week because we believed that the quality of our relationships was the key to the relationships in our church family. We could not expect our people to develop caring, supportive, redemptive relationships if we didn't. We had no choice if we were going to take beauty seriously. Intentional living also involves such things as mutual accountability, regular involvement in personal ministry, and ongoing mutual discipleship.

NEW TESTAMENT QUALIFICATIONS FOR LEADERSHIP

Elders (leaders) are examples to follow; followers are to become like their leaders. They are to talk like their leaders, love like their leaders, care for others like their leaders, build relationships like their leaders, and love and obey God like their leaders. A clear portrait of what a leader should be is given in 1 Timothy 3, Titus 1, and 1 Peter 5. The over twenty qualities listed do not apply merely to church leaders. They are characteristic of every mature child of God. The Bible describes the qualities for the body of Christ; the leader demonstrates or incarnates them. It is important that the messenger *be* good news before he *shares* good news.

As you read the list of qualifications for leaders, imagine that you are a nonbeliever fortunate enough to have a growing friendship with a Christian having these qualities.

Combined List of Qualifications **(1 Timothy 3:1-7; Titus 1:5-10; 1 Peter 5:2)**	
Above reproach (good reputation)	One who manages his own family
Husband of one wife Temperate	Not a recent convert A good reputation with the nonbeliever
Self-controlled	Not overbearing
Respectable Hospitable (lover of strangers)	Loves what is good Upright
Able to teach Not given to much wine	Devout Holds firmly to the trustworthy message
Not violent, but gentle Not quarrelsome	Not quick-tempered Not a lover of money

Quality: Giving the Right Response

There are at least four categories of qualities in this list. First, there are those that have to do with a believer's *responses*. He is to be temperate, not quick-tempered, self-controlled, not violent but gentle, not quarrelsome or overbearing. Under favorable conditions, most people usually meet these requirements. The real test is how we respond under stress.

When the non-Christian observes a believer responding to pressure and pain with a Spirit-controlled response, he is seeing God at work in human experience. Lack of self-control is dangerous. "Just as untaught men leave the Body wounded and bleeding, undisciplined shepherds by their very example, lead God's flock into treacherous territory, causing unstable sheep to stumble and fall. That's why Paul warned his colleagues not to appoint leaders who have a glaring lack of self-control over their personal and social lives."[2]

I won't comment on all the qualities, but I cannot pass up gentleness. A leader is not to be violent, but gentle. This is completely unlike the person who feels he has to stand up for every letter of his legal rights. The gentle person backs away from the letter of the law to preserve its spirit. He stays within the limits of what is moderate and orderly. Gentleness is a true measure of one's spiritual maturity. The violent, divisive person is to be warned and then isolated. Never put a critical, divisive person in leadership. He hasn't earned the right regardless of his training or experience.

Quality: Forming the Right Relationships

A second category of qualities has to do with *relationships* to people and to things. A person's relationship to money is one of the most accurate gauges of his spiritual maturity. God does not want tightwads in places of leadership. Neither the hoarding skinflint nor the wheeling, dealing, fast-buck artist is qualified to lead the flock. Imagine the impact a godly, nonmaterialistic person makes in this materialistic world. God desires that believers give generously and cheerfully of their substance. *The person who is selfish with material things cannot be giving in interpersonal relation-*

ships. The emotional ice of selfishness must be broken before the water of life can flow freely to other thirsty souls. The insatiable desire for money must be brought under scriptural limits.

A one-wife kind of man has eyes for no other woman than the one he married. There is no room for a ladies' man on a leadership team. Many men have never divorced their wives or been "unfaithful," but they are not one-women men, and their wives know it. The mature man is faithful to his wife in his imagination as well as his actions.

Our model leader is also to manage his family well. As Frank Accardy puts it, the New Testament leader must be "family proven." Life's most crucial curriculum is taught in the home. The greatest challenges, the greatest pressures we face are behind the front door. The home is an excellent proving ground for the church because both are families. If a man cannot manage beautifully at home, don't let him get close to leadership in the church. He is to use authority wisely, recognizing that it is derived from God and is a sacred stewardship, not a right. Our leader is never to "lord it over the flock," just as a husband is not to lord it over his wife. The husband's authority, like the authority of Israel's kings, is established by God. Yet most Old Testament kings did not manage Israel well, and many "did evil in the sight of the Lord continuously." The kings who abused authority failed because they were not in total submission to Jehovah, their head. Submission to Christ provides the necessary checks and balances upon the exercise of authority. Without such submission, leadership produces resentment and bitterness.

In his relationship to God, the leader is not to be a *recent convert.* We are often tempted to put new believers with their enthusiasm for the Lord into the leadership limelight. But God is concerned about the quality of the leader's relationship to him. So many of these new converts go up like a rocket and come down like a rock. Paul warns that conceit is a hazard for the new convert, causing him to fall under the devil's judgment (1 Timothy 3:6). Premature promotion often produces a deadly distortion of reality leading to a fall from productive and responsible service. In the King's business only wounded soldiers (veterans) can lead.

They have the patience and endurance for the long haul, and the potential for being worthy models. The new convert cannot model what he has not experienced.

The leader who "loves what is good" (Titus 1:8) has his mind and heart properly focused. He has a strong desire for a worthy, honorable life style. Such a person loves what has moral and practical goodness. According to Paul, the leader is to set an example by doing good (Titus 2:7), to encourage believers to be ready for any good enterprise (Titus 3:1), and to teach believers to devote themselves to doing good (Titus 3:14). The leader must be noted for his love of goodness.

What we love is the truest indication of our character and motivation. Where our treasure is, our heart is also. The leader who loves and pursues anything that is tainted, impure, or unethical is unworthy as a model for Christlikeness. The direction of a man's life and affections must be clearly demonstrated before he can become a model for our Acts 2 Christian. If a world is to be reached for Christ, we need a multitude of men and women armed with good works. Leaders must set the pace in this vital Christian grace.

Quality: Building the Right Reputation

A third category of leadership qualities focuses on *reputation*. The leader is to be above reproach (1 Timothy 3:2, Titus 1:6-7). In the early church, those chosen to wait on tables were required to be men of good reputation (Acts 6:3). Luke said that the brothers "spoke well" of Timothy (Acts 16:2). A person who is above reproach provides no grounds for accusation. He cannot be attacked because of his moral or ethical conduct. This does not mean he has never failed, but that his failures have been acknowledged and dealt with in an honorable, satisfactory manner.

Likewise, a leader is to be respectable (1 Timothy 3:2). Plato used this same term to describe the citizen with a well-ordered life who quietly and faithfully fulfilled his duties. Such a citizen was characterized by tough minded self-management. Under the Lordship of Christ, our leader must demonstrate a godly self-discipline through respectable, honorable behavior. As such, he has credibility with those who know him.

Another critical test of leadership readiness is the reputation one has with nonbelievers (1 Timothy 3:7). Paul says it should be good! No man who is known as a corner-cutting, fast-talking, unethical businessperson has any place in church leadership. Judged by his non-Christian peers, our leader is to receive a good report. His vocabulary must be clean, his concern genuine, his motives honorable, his word good, and his promises true.

Quality: Communicating the Right Revelation

A final category of leadership qualities focuses on the leader's ability to handle divine *revelation*. The leader must have a clear understanding of what Scripture teaches and be mature enough that he can use the Word effectively in both exhortation and refutation (Titus l:9). No novices need apply! Being "able to teach" (1 Timothy 3:2) means the leader can communicate truth in an effective manner; he has the ability to get beyond information to practical implications for living. He can use Scripture to solve personal problems. The way in which he applies Scripture to life is important—he is to teach with authority but not in an authoritarian manner.

The one who is able to teach has learned to communicate truth in a gentle, kind, unquarrelsome way (2 Timothy 2:24-25). His teaching does not lead to quarrels and empty disputes. Unteachable, quarrelsome people are to be handled by our leader with kindness, patience, and gentleness. Sheep are to be led— never driven.

Finally, our model leader is to be hospitable, a "lover of strangers"(1 Timothy 3:2; Titus 1:8). We should remember to extend hospitality to strangers (Hebrews 13:2) and to invite guests home for dinner (Romans 12:13). The leader's home circle is to be an open circle. A man living a Spirit-controlled life, who manages his family well and has a good reputation, is a living, walking miracle. He is a revelation of God's truth to the world. When hurting, seeking souls are allowed to share the warmth and love of Christian hospitality, they are hearing the music of the gospel loud and clear. Here our evangelism strategies often break down. Christians can't handle their humanity. They don't know how to be themselves.

> We have not grasped that it really is okay for us to be who we are when we are with non-Christians, even if we do not have all the answers to their questions or if our knowledge of Scripture is limited. We forget that we are called to be witnesses to what we have seen and know, not to what we do not know. The key is obedience, not a Th.D.[3]

When Ruthe and I were at Dallas Seminary we lived in an apartment building full of every possible type of human being. We shared a building with students, homosexuals, prostitutes, bank robbers, mechanics, divorcees, singles...you name it, we had it. We determined to befriend, love, and hopefully influence them for Christ. On various occasions I had to break up fights, holding the gladiators at gunpoint until the police arrived. On two occasions I arrested sexual perverts. Our lives were threatened. Beer bottles were thrown through our bedroom window in the middle of the night.

In spite of these inconveniences, we spent many hours with these people. They would eat with us, often bringing their beer cans and ash trays. We tried to take at least one couple out to dinner each week. Our home circle was an open circle and they came, they laughed, they cried, they listened, they watched, they talked, and some were saved. They heard the music and asked about the words. At Youngbloods' Fried Chicken Restaurant, Bettye asked, "Joe, we've seen something different about your marriage. We don't know what it is, but we'd like to have it, too."

Authenticity is the key. Christ has liberated us to be genuine, and unless we come to grips with his provision, evangelism becomes a project rather than a life style of beauty. The leader is to be the model of authenticity, the one with a growing reputation as a "lover of strangers."

QUALITIES OF LOVE THAT WORK

There are other qualities essential to effective church leadership. *Leaders must love each other.* This quality needs to be obvious. The men need to be freed to express their affection warmly and openly. Love is built by spending significant, regular time together. Board retreats should be times of personal evaluation where blind spots can be communicated in a spirit of love and acceptance. Leaders must share freely the current state of their spiritual pilgrimage. And they must be open to loving correction if needed. Love speaks the truth; love wounds its object to stimulate growth. Love desires the best for its object and is willing to pay whatever price is necessary to see it achieved. Love holds its object accountable for reaching agreed upon objectives. Leaders are to be brothers and sisters in the fullest and richest sense.

Leaders must exist together in unity. They are to be diligent in maintaining this oneness (Ephesians 4:3). Standing together, they must be willing to sacrifice for each other. Church members must sense the impossibility of pitting one leader against another. They cannot be bought by prestige or position. Jesus Christ is the acknowledged head of the church, and leaders owe their allegiance to him and to each other. Satan's greatest inroads occur where unity is lacking.

Democracy can be dangerous in a church. Decision making based on majority rule can be extremely divisive. Under such a system someone always wins, and someone loses. Personalities enter in, voting blocks develop, politicking is encouraged, and feelings are hurt. If Spirit-controlled men are appointed as leaders, isn't it reasonable to believe that the Spirit can lead them all to the same conclusion? The principle of unanimity (unanimous decision making) encourages unity, builds relationships, and underscores our dependence on the Spirit for wisdom. It also keeps leaders from being "yes men" to their pastor. Just one negative vote stops any action of the group. When this would happen at our church board meetings, we would usually stop everything, drop to our knees in prayer, and seek the mind of Christ. Often the Lord would use this lone vote as a signpost, and we would reverse a decision. We experienced plenty of healthy diversity as we discussed issues, but trusted the Spirit to lead us to consensus. Certainly integrity must supersede unity. God would never call us to compromise our moral convictions to achieve unity. In a healthy body that should not be necessary.

The church leader must know the biblical teachings on the church. With pastors leaving every two or three years, "lay leaders" need to have strong biblical convictions about the nature and purpose of the church. They should invite a pastor to help them fulfill their vision of the church and its local ministry. Such books as *A Church for the Twenty-first Century* by Leith Anderson and *The Body* by Charles Colson should be required reading. They make great topics for a board retreat.

My personal prejudice is that a board should not rotate members every two or three years. It takes at least that long for board members to begin to develop quality relationships and to understand the uniqueness of the church. Furthermore, it puts the pastor in a dangerous position. He becomes the only "permanent" member of the board and often is accountable to no one. He becomes *the* leader, and the rest of the leaders become ineffective. The job of a pastor is to lead with, not lord over. He is the key person to cultivate the environment in which effective leadership qualities can grow. The importance of his role is the substance of the chapter that follows.

Notes

1. Charles B. Williams, *The New Testament in the Language of the People* (Chicago: Moody Press, 1965).

2. Frank Accardy, *A Certain Kind of Man* (Olympia, Wash.: Emmanuel Baptist Church, 1979), 14.

3. Rebecca Pippert, *Pizza Parlor Evangelism* (Downers Grove, Ill.: InterVarsity Press, 1976), 4.

CHAPTER 8

Evangelism and the Pastor

lfred Sloan's definition of an organization as "the lengthened shadow of a man" reinforces that the pastor's behavior is a key to health and renewal in a church. The local church in a large measure is the lengthened shadow of its pastor. Our fourth question focuses on this vital fact.

Question One: What kind of person do we want to deploy into the world?

Question Two: What kind of church makes possible that kind of person?

Question Three: What kind of leadership team makes possible that kind of church?

Question Four: What kind of pastor makes possible that kind of leadership team?

The influence chain in a church looks something like this:

The leader, whoever he may be, is always the focal point for renewal and change within an organization.

WHAT SHOULD A PASTOR BE LIKE?

Unfortunately—or fortunately—we become what we visualize ourselves to be. Often that vision is cultural but not biblical. It is unfortunate for a pastor when church members have predetermined what he should be like and do, especially when their cultural convictions overpower biblical ones. The following advertisement would be funny if it weren't so true.

> WANTED: Minister for growing church. A real challenge for the right man! Opportunity to become better acquainted with people! Applicant must offer experience as shop worker...office manager...educator (all levels, including college)...artist...salesman...diplomat...writer...theologian ...politician...Boy Scout leader...children's worker... minor league athlete...psychologist...vocational counselor...psychiatrist...funeral director...wedding consultant ...master of ceremonies ...circus clown ...missionary ...social worker. Helpful but not essential: experience as a butcher...baker...cowboy...Western Union messenger.

> Must know all about problems of birth, marriage, and death; also conversant with latest theories and practices in areas like pediatrics, economics, and nuclear science.

> Right man will hold firm views on every topic, but is careful not to upset people who disagree. Must be forthright but flexible; returns criticism and backbiting with Christian love and forgiveness. Should have outgoing, friendly disposition at all times. Should be captivating speaker and intent listener....

> Education must be beyond Ph.D. requirements, but always concealed in homespun modesty and folksy talk. Able to sound learned at times but most of the time talks and acts like good-old-Joe. Familiar with literature read by average congregation.

> Must be willing to work long hours, subject to call any time day or night, adaptable to sudden interruption. Will spend at least 25 hours preparing sermon. Additional 10 hours reading books and magazines.

> Applicant's wife must be both stunning and plain, smartly attired but conservative in appearance, gracious and able to get along with everyone, especially women. Must be willing to work in church kitchen, teach Sunday school, babysit, run multilith machine, wait tables, never listen to gossip, never become discouraged.

> Applicant's children must be exemplary in conduct and character; well-behaved, yet basically no different from other children; decently dressed.

Opportunity for applicant to live close to work. Furnished home provided; open-door hospitality enforced. Must be ever mindful the house does not belong to him.

Directly responsible for views and conduct to all church members and visitors, not confined to direction or support from any one person. Salary not commensurate with experience or need; no overtime pay. All replies kept confidential. Anyone applying will undergo full investigation to determine sanity.[1]

Although obviously overstated, the fictitious ad reveals many cultural and biblical expectations the pastor must deal with and attempt to balance. The expectations of people can be a difficult burden. The pastor who attempts to live up to them all risks his health, testimony, and effectiveness. The following is a list of common expectations for the pastor. You determine whether the expectations are cultural or biblical. Not all of the statements will be easily categorized.

Cultural Biblical

Cultural	Biblical	
❏	❏	A pastor should have a personal faith in Christ.
❏	❏	A pastor should live in a parsonage.
❏	❏	A pastor should be married.
❏	❏	A pastor should not be paid well. (This one may fool you.)
❏	❏	A pastor's wife should be a regular church worker.
❏	❏	A pastor's job is to do the work of the ministry.
❏	❏	A pastor's home circle should be an open circle.
❏	❏	A pastor's children should be models for the congregation.
❏	❏	A pastor should lead in prayer each Sunday morning.
❏	❏	A pastor should have a passion for the lost.
❏	❏	Only an ordained minister should preach or teach.
❏	❏	A pastor should not reveal his needs.
❏	❏	A pastor should not associate with non-Christian people and enterprises
❏	❏	A pastor should be competent in all areas of life and ministry.
❏	❏	A pastor should always be available to one and all.

And so it goes. The pressures for conformity are real. Sometimes they are helpful, but often they are devastating.

What kind of pastor does it take to deploy into the world an Acts 2 Christian who is vibrant and alive for Jesus Christ? Ideally, it takes one who personifies all that we have said to this point about our Acts 2 Christian, his local fellowship, and its leaders. Is it any wonder that James says "Not many of you should presume to be teachers" (James 3:1)? It was his half brother who said, "Everyone who is fully trained will be *like* his teacher" (Luke 6:40). The challenge is obvious.

Certainly we expect the pastor to have the qualities of 1 Timothy 3 and Titus 1. These qualities depict a destination the leader progresses toward. No one possesses them perfectly. The pastor should demonstrate that he is consistently developing and cultivating these qualities. We could disqualify most pastors if we took any one of the qualities and pressed hard enough for its mature and effective presence. How many would pass the test of being a lover of strangers? What about managing his own family well? We should not expect perfection. A pastor is like every other believer—another sinner saved by grace who is being progressively conformed to the image of Christ. We do not have a third category. We have lost sinners and sinners saved by grace. Period.

WHAT A PASTOR IS REALLY LIKE

Let me pass along some personal observations about what pastors are really like. Having spoken to hundreds of pastors and having listened to them as they shared their hearts, I know something of what makes them tick. You may be surprised by their genuine humanness. By and large pastors are wonderful people. They really do want to help you. They often agonize over you, desiring to see Christ formed in you. Many of them are discouraged and in some cases defeated. Usually they won't show it, but it's there. Working with a volunteer staff and Sunday Christians is tough. Believers' lack of commitment to Christ and his purposes crushes many of them. Scores leave the pastorate every month because their dream of shepherding a flock of God's people toward maturity turned into a nightmare.

Most feel extremely inadequate. Behind their Sunday morning face they are racked by anxiety and uncertainty. In most cases their seminary training did not prepare them to deal with personal and organizational problems. At best they are skillful in one or two of at least a half dozen necessary skills and abilities. Yet churches expect them to cover all the bases, all at once.

Many pastors are prisoners of other people's expectations. They try desperately to project authenticity in every area of life and ministry. To do this they must continually cover their inauthenticity. Tragically, many feel they should cover it. It is difficult for pastors to cope with their humanity. They need help in being human, in enjoying life, in relating comfortably and naturally to Christians and non-Christians.

Pastors are often lonely. Any leadership position is lonely, but the pastorate can be doubly so. The very word *pastor* presupposes one who leads, who commands, who knows and is in charge in every situation. He's a great guy to be around when the world's caving in, but when the fish are biting he's usually passed over as a fishing buddy, as though he couldn't be one. Many a pastor would love to be included in a fishing trip, but they are seldom invited.

A pastor is often accountable to no one. Most church constitutions establish some legal accountability, but that's not what I'm referring to. Few pastors have a "pastor" (layman or otherwise) who serves as their priest and confidant. Eight out of ten say they do not have a single friend. No one holds them accountable in their spiritual growth, family relations, and ministry responsibilities.

The pastorate can be an attractive haven for lazy people. In seminary I heard J. Vernon McGee state that laziness was the number one sin of pastors. I have never forgotten his words. Businessmen have schedules to meet and quotas to produce. Regular evaluations are scheduled and completed. Performance feedback is readily available. The nature of the pastoral ministry is such that accountability is rare and difficult. How do you measure spirituality? Without some type of accountability a pastor can put in as much as a sixty-hour week and still be lazy or ineffective.

Some spend hours doing unproductive things. Others are efficient but not effective. In many cases the pastor can use help in time management and principles of organization and administration. The other extreme, of course, is the pastor who has a need to "burn himself out" for Jesus . . . usually sacrificing his home life for ministry.

Pastors' wives are often hurting—silently. They are the walking wounded. Many of the books on being a pastor's wife should be burned. Let them be themselves, have their own friends, stay home from church if they feel like it, and never get involved in the ministry of the "church gathered" if their gifts are elsewhere. Let their children be children. Let them spill their milk, kick up their heels, or try their wings like any other red-blooded young person. If necessary, sell the parsonage and let them live like real people in a real world.

Many pastors are underpaid. As a general rule, a pastor should make as a minimum what the average person in his congregation makes. He should live like his parishioners—his food, clothes, car, home, and retirement plan should be comparable to theirs. His salary should not be a weapon to control or manipulate him. It should be freely and graciously given with no strings attached. Certainly "God will provide," and the pastor is to live by faith, but he isn't the only one who is to live by faith!

The freedom to express love is denied to many pastors. They may feel it, but often cultural conditioning and faulty seminary instruction have rendered them incapable of communicating it. Start a revolution. If your pastor is this way, get a bunch of your people involved in a plot to solve the problem. Each Sunday for eight weeks walk up to him at the end of the service and give him a big hug. Tell him you love him. He'll never be the same again!

Many pastors struggle with their devotional life. For some it's almost nonexistent. Some have abandoned prayer because of repeated discouragement. Others have allowed sermon preparation to become a substitute for personal time with the Lord. They often feel guilty about this. They need your understanding and prayer.

Few pastors have any non-Christian friends. In most cases they are not reaching their neighborhoods for Christ. This lack of effective contact with non-Christians colors their understanding of separation and their practice of evangelism. Many excuse their lack of neighborhood penetration because some people do find Christ as a result of their preaching and counseling ministry. Most pastors need lots of help in building bridges to their non-Christian contacts.

Sometimes pastors can become very threatened people. Other ministries threaten them. Some cannot trust laymen. Others will not take constructive criticism. I have seen pastors withdraw from their staff until there is no longer any significant contact. Staff members who were friends and fellow workers are abandoned. In some cases, the pastor cannot handle success. He begins to believe his press clippings and the "glorifying of the worm" ceremony at the church door following the service.

Pastors by the dozens leave the ministry each year because of moral failure. Uphold them before the Lord because the temptations are real and opportunities for transgression abound. God has given to the church gifted men called pastors. They are to be loved, respected, encouraged, and uplifted. They are human and face all the temptations of every other human being. They have their faults, fears, and inadequacies. Allow them the freedom to succeed and to fail. Support them and challenge them. Care for them and in love confront them. Your love and support may revolutionize them and in the process change the very personality of your church.

SOME MARKS OF MATURITY FOR A PASTOR

To help identify the kind of shepherd who stimulates beauty, let's look now at some marks of maturity for a pastor. These are goals to shoot for, a direction to move. Since pupils are to become like their teachers, they are really goals for all of us.

The Mark of an Expanding Faith

Faith is that God-given ability to take the promises of God out of mothballs and apply them to the challenges of everyday living.

Men of faith dream God-sized dreams and then move out to transform those dreams into reality.

God has said that without faith, it is impossible to please him (Hebrews 11:6). Pleasing him is believing him. Faith as *belief* is affirming who he is while faith as *action* is responsible behavior in the light of who he is and what he has promised. Sometimes it is behavior which overcomes overwhelming odds. By faith men of God "conquered kingdoms...shut the mouths of lions...became powerful in battle" (11:33-34). More often it is a tenacious behavior which endures in the midst of intense struggle and personal loss. "Others were tortured and refused to be released, so that they might gain a better resurrection" (11:35). Some accepted joyfully the seizure of their property because they knew they had a better and an eternal possession (10:34). Faith is not shrinking back, whether one faces *opportunity* or *oppression*.

Our Lord warned against the leaven of the Sadducees (rationalism). Rationalism—eliminating the supernatural—becomes the great enemy of faith. The deceptive thing about the leaven of the Sadducees is its reasonableness. Rationalism is reasonable and safe. Faith often appears unreasonable and risky. It was both unreasonable and risky for Peter to attempt to walk on water. It was unreasonable for Noah to build a boat, for Abraham to expect a son, for Moses to abandon the prestige of Egypt, and for George Mueller to care for orphans.

We must all grow in faith if we are to please him. Certainly we want to do that! The great faith chapter (Hebrews 11) gives us three clues for faith building.

1. Belief in the Invisible. These faith giants saw through the problems of the natural world to a supernatural Being. They saw him who is invisible (11:27). The writer to the Hebrews exhorts us to do the same: "Let us run with perseverance the race marked out for us. Let us fix our eyes on Jesus, the author and perfecter of our faith" (12:1-2). Our eyes must move from the waves to the Master of the waves, from the storm to the Savior, from the fire to the Father. Abraham left the familiar and went out into the unfamiliar, the new, the untested, the uncharted, because he saw that God was the architect and builder of his future (11:10). Cultivation of our relationship with him who is invisible is the first key for building faith.

2. Faith in What Has Been Promised. The heroes of faith not only saw him who was invisible, but they welcomed his promises from a distance (11:13). As we cultivate a relationship with God we are able to claim with assurance (faith) the promises which grow out of that relationship. Sarah was enabled to conceive because Abraham believed God would be faithful to what he had promised (11:11). He believed God was reliable. Our pastor must know both the *person* of God and *the promises* of God if he is to be a man of faith.

Two things hinder this process: 1) A lack of knowledge of the promises of God, and 2) a lack of faith in the person and character of God. Men and women of faith welcome the promises of God from a distance. That is, their major expectations are in the future, in life beyond the veil. Moses claimed the promises of God and turned his back on the prestige, power, and wealth of Egypt because "he was looking ahead to his reward" (11:26). Others joyfully accepted the confiscation of their property knowing that they had "better and lasting possessions" (10:34). They will be winners; they will not be ashamed for the choices they made because God is faithful, his promises are true, and "he has prepared a city for them" (11:16). An expanding faith must be marked by confidence in God's promises.

3. Living a Faith Life Style . A real winner feels the gold medal around his neck before he enters the race. So should the pastor. He should run to win, and motivate by his courageous example a multitude to run with him. The promises of God should be the fabric of his future. Faith begins with the *person* of God, moves to his *promises,* and then to a *pattern* for living. Ours is a living faith and a faith to be lived.

Faith's Process

Cultivation of belief in the Person of God → Confidence in the Promises of God → Commitment to the Pattern of God

There is a faith life style summed up in Hebrews 11:13:

> All these people were still living by faith when they died. They did not receive the things promised; they only saw them and welcomed them from a distance. And they admitted that they were aliens and strangers on earth.

Pastors of all people must make this confession. It is the Magna Carta of Christian living. These heroes of the faith abandoned any hope of ultimate fulfillment in this life. They determined to ever be foreigners in their own countries, to live as aliens in their own land.

No city on this earth, no geographical location, no second home in the mountains has foundations which will last. We should abandon all hope of being satisfied and fulfilled with what is temporal. Our heartache is eternal, and no temporal bicarbonate will ease it. Nothing less than seeing Jesus face to face and dwelling in his presence will ever satisfy our deep longing. It's a longing for home, and this world will never be our home.

Much of the Christian community acts as though this world is its home. Materialism is rampant. We have followed the gospel of the worldling who hopes that by doubling the cost of his new home he can double his happiness. This perverted gospel cripples the impact of countless Christians. The visible mark of faith is an alignment with an eternal home which creates an attitude and life style marked by its contrast with the secularism of our day. This alignment refocuses everything else. It changes our goals and objectives. It redirects our gifts and abilities and resources. It redefines our mission. Suddenly eternity with the Lord is everything, and his purposes become critical as we prepare for that great day. The "alien and stranger" lives for the possibility of hearing his Master say, "Well done, good and faithful servant." Like Moses, he looks forward to the reward.

Pastors must be examples to the church of total stewardship. They should richly enjoy all that God has given, *but their heavenly citizenship should be obvious.* The deceitfulness of wealth, of any treasure but God himself, is a dangerous time bomb. Some pastors err in the other direction. They parade their poverty and continually let their needs be known, and then praise God for his wonderful provision. Be careful, and pray for balance.

Faith is the essential ingredient that pleases God. Faith is fueled as the pastor cultivates the presence of God. As D. L. Moody used to say, "I am a leaky vessel, and I need to keep under the tap." Faith is freed as the pastor develops confidence in the promises of God. It is properly focused as he adopts God's pattern of living. The man of faith is an alien sent by God as an agent of reconciliation. An ad in a secular magazine stated, "Once you discover you can change the world you'll never be the same." How true! Faith moves mountains.

The Marks of a Positive Ministry

Faith and hope are inseparable friends. The gospel itself is literally "good news." A pastor should both be and communicate good news. It's largely a matter of attitude. Many pastors gravitate toward a negative, critical, condemning pattern of life and ministry. Such a life style is not from God.

> It is often thought that the Christian faith is a deprivation of joy in living, or that it is a mere pattern of religious observances, or that it is a hairsplitting system of beliefs. Christianity does involve some of these elements but they are only incidental. The modern evangelist has to sell the biblical point of view that the Christian faith is God's way to undreamed of personal fulfillment. This will necessitate a shift to a more positive point of view in order to change this false but popular image of Christianity.[2]

Pastors need to be ministers of hope. It should permeate their lives and their preaching. Recently I heard a speaker say that the one who brings the most hope gains the most authority. That's an amazing and scary thought. Lenin came with a message of hope and changed the world. As his "Utopia" unfolded, people gave everything, even their very lives, to further the cause. People rally around the bearer of hope and submit themselves to him. Hope is a vital quality for pastors.

Peter reminds us that we are to be ready to give an answer, with "gentleness and respect," to everyone who asks us the reason for our *hope* (1 Peter 3:15). This is not "pumping sunshine."

Ministry is tough. It involves heartache, tragedy, and despair. The shepherd needs to have a faith which produces a hope that encourages, comforts, and strengthens even as the dark clouds gather. Those who worship Jesus Christ have reason for hope.

A ministry founded on and giving rise to hope is composed of several positive factors:

1. An Unveiled Face—Authenticity. One of the joys of the new covenant is that the veils can come off. Moses came down from the mountain and veiled his face so that his people could not see his glory fade away. In 2 Corinthians 3:12-18 Paul tells us that we no longer have to function as did Moses. When one "turns to the Lord, the veil is taken away" (3:16). Let's not bring back what God has taken away. The Christian pilgrimage is not one sanctifying experience after which we put on the veil. We don't reach a point where a veil becomes necessary. The longer we walk with him, the less a veil should be needed. Paul encourages us to look at him with unveiled face as we "are being transformed into his likeness with ever-increasing glory" (3:18).

People are attracted by authenticity. The pastor must guard himself against accepting the illusions, fantasies, or distorted expectations of his congregation. Integrity is the critical element. It is so easy to deceive from the pulpit, to preach about things we have not experienced and do not consistently practice. It is so easy to overstate, to play on guilt, and to imply that we solved a particular problem long ago. If we haven't and imply that we have (often by what we don't say), we are inauthentic.

2. A Diligent Student of the Word. The demands of ministry are great, but they must not take the pastor away from the Book. Since when should the pastor do the calling, teach Sunday school, chair three or four committees, fold the bulletins, oversee the youth ministries, plan the retreats, and on and on? His job has never been to *do* the work of the ministry. He is to equip *others* to do it.

Bible study, however, is hard work. There are plenty of things to keep a pastor "busy" and to provide an excuse for his lack of preparation. Poor preaching keeps most churches poor. Poor preaching in most cases is the result of poor priorities and procrastination. The minister who is going to build a contagious congregation must handle truth skillfully, knowing that truth is the foundation of beauty.

Besides direct study of Scripture, the pastor must continue to learn. Seminars, books, retreats, and significant fellowship should have high priority in his schedule. Many secular management training programs are excellent. Each local church should set aside a substantial sum for its pastor's continuing enrichment. It is money well spent.

3. A Liberator of the Body. The marvelous doctrine of reconciliation helps us see that ultimately evangelism is what Jesus Christ is doing through his church to reach his world. The pattern looks like this. At Christ's incarnation, God was "reconciling the world to himself in Christ" (2 Corinthians 5:19). Since Christ ascended to his Father's right hand, the Father "has committed to us the message of reconciliation. We are therefore Christ's ambassadors, as though God were making his appeal through us" (5:19-20). That's what Christ is doing today. He entreats a lost world to be reconciled through his church, which is his body. Christ sows his good seed (beautiful seed) in the world, where his work is to take place.

The pastor must focus his church outward, not inward. His motto should be, "When the saints, go marching *out!*" The church is not a holy huddle, it is a task force whose primary focus must always be the "fields ripe for harvest." Unfortunately, bigger buildings, larger programs, and more staff dictate church mission. We must justify our large expenditures, and the basic evangelism strategy becomes herding fish toward our expensive, stained-glass trap. Instead, the church should be God's family extending itself to meet needs in the name of Jesus. Evangelism is what Jesus is *actually doing* through the preaching, the worship and fellowship, and the service of the church.

The pastor more than any other individual determines the character of the church's preaching, fellowship, worship, and service. The content and style of his preaching is critical to the church's health and beauty. If a church is to be *a learning center,* the pastor must make diligent preparation so that what is delivered is biblical, balanced, relevant, and liberating. Likewise, the pastor is the key to liberating the church to be *a healing communion* as he gives himself to building up the body so that it moves toward health. The pastor is also the key to whether or not the church is free to worship and to respond as a family to the presence of God in its midst. Finally, the service of the church is conditioned by the pastor's vision (or lack of it). Liberating a congregation to be *God's* people in service can be threatening. It often involves a rethinking of the pastoral and leadership roles. In most cases it means seeking a lower profile and elevating the gifts and abilities of others.

Jesus desires to explode himself through the lives of his people and do greater works than he did while on earth. He wants once again to touch the untouchables, feed the hungry, bring light where there is darkness and life where there is death. He wants to invite the thirsty—whoever they are, wherever they are—to discover living water. In the counsels of eternity, God decided for a time to link himself (and in a sense limit himself) to the frailties of his creatures. Why he has not evangelized with the hosts of heaven we do not know. What we do know is that Jesus' mission today is done *through us,* his ambassadors. We are now members of the second incarnation called to make visible the invisible God. His impact, his mission, is linked to our obedience and vision. If we draw limits he has not drawn, he becomes limited in his outreach. If our hearts have no compassion for the lost, we neglect our commission and Christ's mission is aborted.

Who do you think God wants to use to reach your neighborhood? Is he doing it? Why not? Pastor, you are God's instrument to set people free—to encourage them, to liberate them, to give them your blessing to mark the lost for Christ. It may mean you will have to change your attitudes toward the unsaved. You may need to realign your understanding of separation with biblical truth. Perhaps you will have to eliminate some programs, change the thrust and tone of your preaching, focus again on the essentials, and start reaching your own neighborhood. People may need to be encouraged *not* to attend the programs and activities of the church so they can spend time with the unsaved. Your church may need, with your firm leadership, to move out into the community and serve it. Neglected widows may need help, injustice in your community may need to be confronted, programs may need to be implemented to care for the poor and needy...with no strings attached. You may need to brainstorm with your leadership team about where Jesus would go in your community to meet needs, and then direct resources and people into that area. Christianity in action under qualified leadership is always effective evangelistically.

4. A Builder of Men. Men attract men, especially in a church context. A primary part of the pastor's job is the building of men. To nudge men on toward maturity takes time and commitment. His must help others to minister—not do the work of ministry himself.

> The minister is like the foreman in a machine shop, or the coach of a team. He does not do all the work, nor does he make all the plays. (Though he is a *working* foreman and a *playing* coach!) If a man can't operate a lathe, the foreman rolls up his sleeves and shows him how. If a player can't carry out an assignment, the coach demonstrates how to make the play.[3]

Even though the pastor is a shepherd who loves the entire body, a ministry to men must have a special place in his heart. While in the pastorate I met with at least five groups of men each week. I met one on one with a dentist friend, with two other board members, with a group of twenty or thirty businessmen, with the entire board, and with the pastoral staff (seven men). Although the group dynamics were different, the purposes were similar. With mutual accountability we shared the Word, prayer, schedules, and relationships. Each year, at my request, the board of elders met without me to evaluate my ministry, my marriage and family, and anything else they desired. This information, often painful, was shared in love and resulted in growth and encouragement. It also set a precedent. As they saw the value of evaluation, the board members requested that each of them be evaluated too. (A sample evaluation form you may want to adapt for your church's use is included in the appendix.)

We as a board recognized our need to be a redemptive community. We structured our weekly board meetings so that the first hour focused on instruction and worship. Board members rotated the teaching assignment among themselves. I spent hours working with some of the men helping prepare them to preach and teach. What an exciting experience to sit on the front row as one of them delivers the morning message! Men, help your pastor by being honest with him. I remember so well the evening a man in my congregation said to me, "Joe, you've been my pastor for two years. I'm disappointed you haven't built into my life more effectively." It was a time of soul searching . . . and growth. You may need to pose a similar question to your pastor to nudge him into one of his most important responsibilities. An effective pastor builds into his leaders to establish the base for a healthy and attractive ministry. Before a church is ready to add members, it must increase the quality and quantity of its leadership. A wise pastor learns how to be a builder of men, then makes this challenge central to his ministry.

5. A Family Specialist. Focus on the family! Target sermons regularly on marriage and family living. Take advantage of the excellent video series and printed materials available. People are hurting desperately in this area. Meet these needs and evangelism problems are practically solved. If your church cannot accept the wreckage of broken homes and shattered dreams, it is not a place where Jesus lives. Your church should be the greatest garbage dump in town—a place where the broken, oppressed, misplaced, abandoned, and unloved can come and find a family where they are accepted and loved…as is. "As is" people are Jesus' kind of people. The Pharisees despised them. They still do. "As is" people become great disciples and great soul winners. Those who have been forgiven the most love the most.

The effective church ministers effectively to families because it is a family. Pastor, you're the key. Father the fatherless, rebuke the offenders, encourage the discouraged, rejoice with those who rejoice, and weep, weep, weep. If your heart is not broken by broken people, you don't have Jesus' heart. If your heart is not compelled to go when lost men stumble in darkness, you don't have Jesus' heart. Pray that his mission will recapture the hearts of his children and of their leaders.

6. A Careful Planner. The old adage is true: If you fail to plan, you plan to fail. A goal is a statement of faith about the future. Visions remain visions unless goals are established as steps to the visions' realization. Aim at nothing and you'll hit it every time. A careful planner simply puts a foundation under his fantasy.

Some years ago I put together a document which has been very influential in shaping my life. It contains my personal objectives, goals, and standards. I established objectives and goals in five areas: spiritual, intellectual, physical, family, and ministry. Objectives became broad statements of purpose. Suppose one objective in my spiritual life is to be conformed to the image of Christ. That is a broad, unmeasurable purpose. To achieve it I must establish several goals. One goal would be to maintain a regular Bible study program. Another might be to develop a significant prayer life. Reading Christian biographies could be another goal. If I meet these goals I will be well on my way toward my objective of Christ-likeness. Unfortunately, these goals are still too general and unmeasurable. Therefore, I must establish standards to quantify my goals and make them measurable. Here is a sample:

I. Objective: To be conformed to the image of Christ.

   A. Goal: Regular Bible study

      1. Standard: 30 minutes each day in Bible study

      2. Standard: 10 minutes each day in devotional literature

      3. Standard: Weekly reading of pertinent journals, such as Christianity *Today*

   B. Goal: Develop a significant prayer life

      1. Standard: 30 minutes each day

      2. Standard: Written requests with answers recorded

      3. Standard: Daily prayer with wife and family

      4. Standard: Daily prayer with staff

   C. Goal: Read significant Christian biographies

      1. Standard: One biography per month

Such an exercise is invaluable. The more you plan, the more efficient is your time spent in working. Perhaps the greatest value of planning is the "self-fulfilled prophecy" effect Planning plants seeds which enable visions to grow into realities. Planning is simply taxing the mind to solve the problems that keep us from a fruitful future. Not to plan is not to set in operation the incredible resources of the human mind, a resource which when linked with faith can move mountains. A man of vision plans...so does an effective shepherd.

Our fifth and final question is one only the pastor can answer: "What changes must take place in the life of the pastor to make him that kind of a person?" It is a critical question. Pastors need the insight and the feedback of their leaders to answer it effectively. The question cannot be answered unless it's asked. My prayer is that many pastors will take the risk...and ask.

Notes

1. William McRae, *The Dynamics of Spiritual Gifts* (Grand Rapids: Zondervan Publishing House, 1976), 123-24.

2. James Jauncey, *Psychology for Successful Evangelism* (Chicago: Moody Press, 1972), 39.

3. Leighton Ford, *The Christian Persuaders* (New York: Harper & Row, 1966), 49.

Part 3

Evangelism and You

CHAPTER 9

Your Home and Evangelistic Bible Studies

*T*he laughter and boisterous behavior of the noisy crowd, lined up two or three deep around the bar, drowned out the TV as it droned on and on. A gray-haired, distinguished-looking man elbowed his way through the crowd until he reached the counter. Pounding on it with his fists he quieted the crowd. Attention gained, he blurted out, "Let's talk about Jesus Christ!" Somehow nobody wanted to talk. Sophisticated conversationalists who only moments before couldn't get a word in edgewise were hard put to get a word out. All talk ceased when Christ's name was introduced into the conversation. Tongues got tied, palms got sweaty, hearts palpitated, and faces turned crimson.

In a Sunday morning sermon I had challenged the congregation to walk up to a group of strangers and invite them to talk about Jesus Christ. My friend, a bold and courageous new Christian, accepted the challenge and proved a point. The song is right: "There's just something about that name." No other name creates that universal response. It is highly unlikely that anyone would feel that sense of unrest, threat, or embarrassment if the conversation focused upon Mohammed, Buddha, or Joseph Smith.

Non-Christians aren't the only ones who feel embarrassed talking about Jesus Christ. Christians do, too! Besides wanting to vanish, run, or hide, embarrassed people are often unable to act appropriately. They often can't think logically or act rationally. Embarrassment usually comes when circumstances reveal inadequacy or inappropriate behavior.

Embarrassment stops some believers from sharing because they don't yet feel perfect. Fearing that the non-Christian will spot some flaws, these believers keep their distance so as not to be hypocritical." (For some this is a legitimate concern—they *are* hypocritical.) Regardless of our attempts to appear otherwise, the world knows we are not perfect. If we would allow them, they might be surprised to see that we are at least making progress in a positive, wholesome direction instead of "advancing progressively backwards" (T. S. Eliot) with the rest of society.

The topic of this chapter could be described as "How to Perform Heart Surgery Without the Patient Knowing It!" Perhaps this chapter will be an encouragement to some of our "embarrassed brethren." Believe it or not, your home could be the scene of divine surgery in which the cutting power of God's Word is used to penetrate spiritual scar tissue, laying bare men's hearts to the demands of a holy God. My wife and I have been involved in numerous evangelistic Bible studies under every conceivable circumstance. Dozens of people have discovered Christ as they interacted with others around God's principles found in Scripture. And we have found certain musts for the evangelistic effectiveness of these studies.

Let me first warn you, though, that there is a big difference between an *evangelistic* home Bible study and a home Bible study. The two do not mix. I am sure you know of Bible studies where an overzealous Sister Maude or Brother Jim showed up ready to do battle. It was not long before the discussion turned from the simple ABCs of the faith to the eschatological implications of the ten horns of the beast in Daniel 7. What started out to be an evangelistic Bible study turned into a society for protecting, preserving, and propagating pet theological hobby horses.

INGREDIENTS FOR AN EFFECTIVE EVANGELISTIC STUDY

For your home to be a successful context for evangelism, you must adopt a distinctive philosophy that will encourage the likes of Maude and Jim to join another group capable of appreciating their theological insights. In the long run, this will profit your purposes of evangelism as well as steer Maude and Jim to the right group.

A Proper View of Separation

In order to work with unsaved people, we must have *a healthy understanding of separation.* Biblical separation is not simply avoiding sin, nor is it isolation from unredeemed mankind; rather it is separation *from* acts of personal sin and separation *unto* God.

Some churches are similar to a department store where all the employees arrive at the prescribed time, lock the doors, and then sell merchandise to each other all day. To do any good, salt not only has to get out of the shaker, it must also come into contact with the food. Otherwise, it's useless.

A Trust in God's Word

An effective evangelistic strategy *must place confident trust in the power and authority of God's Word.* When people interact with its truths things happen...often unexpected things. Unbelievers find themselves at the foot of the cross and wonder how they got there.

God is not dependent upon our tactics and devices. Consequently we can leave behind our sanctimonious speech, our furrowed brow, our pointed finger, and our spiritual 2 x 4s (not to mention our string ties and Herbert Hoover collars).

How freeing and refreshing it is to bring people under the healthy teaching of the Word and leave the results to God. If we trust the convicting power of God's Spirit, our strategy can be "low pressure, long range."

A Wholesome Atmosphere

The effective study must have a carefully cultivated atmosphere. This provides the context in which the gospel content has its greatest impact. In the first three or four sessions, atmosphere is probably more important than content. We're talking about beauty again.

Create an atmosphere where the non-Christian feels at home. The evangelistic study is for nonbelievers, not believers. If believers are in the majority and insensitive to the group dynamics, they will soon drive the non-Christians away. The non-Christian needs to feel it is *his* group because he senses other people like him are present. I watched a group of thirty-five non-Christians diminish to practically zero because of the rudeness and insensitivity of some uninvited Christians who "crashed" the study. The only Christians who should be present are those who are bringing their non-Christian friends.

Even under these circumstances, it is best to set down a few ground rules. First, the purpose of the study is evangelism. Second, the non-Christian must feel comfortable and welcome. Third, most of the discussion should involve non-Christians. As a general rule, the Christian should avoid active participation in the discussion. Fourth, avoid religious clichés. Fifth, avoid discussion of various churches and denominations. Sixth, resist the temptation to straighten out the participants' doctrinal views that are not central to salvation. The issue is Jesus Christ, not infant baptism, total immersion, the inspiration of Scripture, pretribulationalism, or Post Toasties. Seventh, refrain from bringing up all kinds of parallel passages. As a general rule the study should confine itself to one passage. Anyone can make significant observations on five or six verses. However, once the "resident experts" start spouting off other passages, the non-Christian realizes he is outgunned and out of place. Eighth, as a general rule, the Christian participants should avoid giving advice or sharing pious platitudes and spiritual Band-aids. If they share, they should focus on their *personal experience of the truth,* not an untested list from some seminar or textbook. Ninth, avoid the temptation to press for premature decisions. Tenth, the Christians should avoid the "holy huddle" syndrome. Some of your best friends may be there, but your mission is to reach out in love to the non-Christian. He must be made to feel special. He is!

Create an atmosphere in which the nonbeliever feels free to participate. One way to encourage participation is to build the entire study around three to four key questions. For example, when I teach on the story of the woman at the well, I normally divide the group into two or three smaller groups, appoint leaders (usually non-Christians), and let them wrestle with four questions. What a thrill it is to see them interact with God's powerful Word. After twenty minutes or so, I call the groups back together and let each group report its findings. We have lots of fun in the process. You want to know what the question are?

1. Describe the physical appearance of the woman at the well. What did she look like?

2. Describe the emotional condition of this woman who had been rejected by five men and was living with a sixth.

3. What did Jesus offer as a solution to her problem?

4. Does his solution have any relevance to the needy people in our world? If so, how does it become operational in our experience?

The questions about her appearance spark lots of humorous discussion. To have six men, she must have been pretty attractive. On the other hand, having put up with six men…

Imagine the emotional state of one who sought love, security, and affection from five husbands and struck out. A woman's number one fear is to be used and abandoned. Five times she realized her worst fear. Believe me, there will be some identification going on in your group. The Samaritan woman has legions of contemporary brothers and sisters still trying to ease eternal heartaches with temporal bicarbonates. What an exciting time it is to hear them discuss the relevance of Christ's offer of thirst-quenching water. Sometimes they almost lead themselves to the Lord!

Another way to encourage the participation of the non-Christian is to compliment him for his observations. We often don't know what to get excited about. It may be a vanilla, model T Ford-truth he discovers…one we've known since church camp days. But if it's brand new to him, *get excited!* It's a sin to bore people with God's Word. Encourage the participation of all in the discussion. Don't let one or two answer all the questions. Let them know you are not afraid of silence. Some people get nervous when no one responds and feel they must talk even if they have nothing to say. If someone persists in dominating, talk to him after the session. Try to keep from becoming the "answer man." Often it's good to throw the question back to the group by asking, "What do some of you think?"

Another way to encourage participation is to *write down key observations* made by group members and write their names beside their observations. When you summarize the group's conclusions at the end of the meeting, mention both the observation and the person who made it. "Susan noted that Jesus was sensitive to the woman's need for something to satisfy her desire for security." Participation is encouraged by an open, free, unthreatened leader. Group members may be hostile. Some are present under duress. Others may delight in asking sticky questions. If you don't know the answer, admit it. "Hey Jim, that's a great question. Let me think about it. I'm not prepared to answer it right now. I'll bounce it off my pastor and get back with you next week."

Participation is encouraged by variety. The worst method is the same method. Discussions, tapes, videos, role playing, skits, and questions and answers are but a few possible methods. Be creative! People love it.

Create an atmosphere in which the nonbeliever feels loved and accepted. Much of the previous discussion is pertinent to assuring an atmosphere of love and acceptance, but we can do more. The expectation of most non-Christians who dare to venture into anything "religious" is to be judged and condemned. They often feel awkward, guilty, and ill at ease. "The unchurched person often has a built-in expectation of being rebuffed. He thinks we can smell his sin in his clothes."[1] Unfortunately, their expectations are often not unfounded. The sensitive, caring, loving Christian should therefore go out of his way to make sure the non-Christian feels welcomed and loved. If he does, he'll never recover. Group love and acceptance seems to be a basic need of the human heart. As they feel accepted, they have "a built-in inclination to accept the group's religious beliefs even before they know them. It becomes an easy step to graduate from the social functions to the religious activities."[2]

A congenial, accepting atmosphere eases communication and

increases the impact of truth. The host and hostess are often the key to the success of the group. 1) Effective hosts have the gift of hospitality, the ability to make people feel welcome and secure. 2) They understand the purpose and philosophy of the evangelistic study. 3) Effective hosts have a significant number of non-Christian friends. 4) They do not demand regenerate behavior from unregenerate people. 5) They learn the names of the group members. There is no sweeter music than one's own name! 6) Effective hosts are skilled at drawing people into conversation. They realize the importance of tying people together into webs of friendships. 7) Effective hosts are sensitive to people's needs at the study. Such routine things as temperature, ventilation, lighting, ash trays, and extra Bibles are on the host's mental checklist.

Exposure, Exposure, Exposure

A final ingredient for effective evangelism in these studies comes as you continue to spend time with the group. Put in three words, it is *exposure, exposure,* and *exposure.* Christians in the study should make their home circle an open circle. They need to take the initiative in setting up dinner engagements, recreational outings, and other group activities which will allow the non-Christian to hear more of the music of the gospel. He needs to know that Christians can laugh, play, and have fun.

We have found that a potluck about four or five weeks into a study is a great way to strengthen relationships and build bridges. The group members enjoyed setting aside an evening just for food and fellowship. Some of God's most significant work takes place around a dinner table.

Group activities build esprit de corps and tie people together. A weekend retreat can be extremely effective in opening people to the gospel. Nothing can compare to getting away for several days with a mixture of sensitive Christians and searching non-Christians. It's dynamite. A word of caution: Focus on fun and fellowship. Resist the temptation to dump the whole load on your captive audience. The keys are balance, common sense, and a yieldedness to the Spirit's direction.

SUGGESTIONS FOR THE FORMAT

An evangelistic study need not be rigidly formatted, but there are some general suggestions for planning such a gathering. Some type of refreshments should be included. The informal chatting around the refreshment table helps break down barriers. The refreshment time also provides a sounding board for personal reactions to the Bible study and to initiate conversation about spiritual things. Refreshments should be served at the *beginning* of the class time. Besides establishing a congenial atmosphere, it allows a latecomer to arrive fifteen minutes late and still be on time for the study itself. Refreshments are still available at the conclusion of the study for those who desire to stay longer. The hostess must resist the temptation to supply the refreshments each week. Let others volunteer and sign them up ahead of time. It helps assure their continued presence at the study (at least the night they bring the goodies). It also helps build the sense of it being "their group."

Utilize the phone. "You have not because you phone not" should be your motto. Personal contact goes a long way toward assuring the continued participation of group members. Make every effort to begin and end on schedule. If the study is to go until 9:00 P.M., stop at 9:00 no matter how exciting the discussion. It's better to leave them longing than loathing. A good group leader knows how important it is to stop at a high point rather than trying to get extra mileage out of it.

Normally I close a study something like this. "Well, gang, it's nine o'clock—time to quit. Some of you have baby-sitters and need to get home right away. However, some of you may want to stay and continue our discussion. Let's take a five minute break. Grab a cup of coffee, and if any of you want to continue our discussion or have further questions, I'll be happy to stay and be of help." Often half the group will hang around and continue to talk about the implications of the study. These dialogues sometimes last several hours. Sometimes the most significant spiritual advances are made during these unstructured, informal bull sessions. Be especially sensitive to those who hang around and "straighten up the chairs." Often such a person wants to talk about spiritual things and doesn't know how to begin. But remember, it is important that you keep your word and end the formal study right on time.

Have extra Bibles available. Many never take their Bibles to church, much less to a Bible study. They might be embarrassed to be seen with one. Suggest that next week they "dust off their Bible, wrap it in a plain brown wrapper, and bring it." They will. Once you get to know some of the non-Christians, invite different ones to read the passage you're studying.

Use humor freely. Many non-Christians are delighted to discover that Christians can laugh and have a good time. Don't be afraid to laugh at yourself. And use personal illustrations when they are appropriate. Don't, however, limit them to your successes. Often your failures have much more impact. Whatever you do, don't take yourself too seriously! Relax.

Pray for each class member daily. Make a list and encourage each participating Christian to do the same. You are in a spiritual battle for people's souls, and to succeed, the study must be undergirded with prayer. Normally, however, I do not begin or end the study time with prayer. This will vary with the circumstances, but most often non-Christians aren't ready for it.

Frequent evaluation is important to assure quality studies. If you are leading the group, ask two or three key people to evaluate your leadership and the group's interest and response. Never assume motivation. In every group session the leader must overcome an initial inertia. A good story or a personal experience shared at the beginning can break the ice and get the group rolling. Pay attention to how the group session ends. An effective leader summarizes the group's discussion in such a way that the members sense that significant observations were made and significant conclusions were reached. There needs to be a sense of resolution or closure. Otherwise, many conclude that the group simply pooled its ignorance.

As mentioned earlier, during the study jot down significant observations and the name of the person who contributed it. Use these observations as the basis for your summary. Not only will it reinforce the important truths, it will affirm the group members.

Finally, vary the content according to the needs of the people. Here are a dozen suggested topics:

1. The home.
2. An overview of the Bible.
3. The inspiration and the reliability of Scripture.
4. Evolution and the biblical view of creation.
5. The Bible and modern culture.
6. Contemporary theology and Scripture.
7. Individual book studies, such as John, Mark, or Romans.
8. Biblical characters.
9. Basic Bible doctrine.
10. "Twenty difficult questions" (Are the heathen lost? Is the Bible inspired? and so on)
11. A series centered around a significant Christian book, such as *Mere Christianity* (Lewis); *Escape from Reason* (Schaeffer); *Where Is God When It Hurts?* (Yancey); *Christian Basics* (Stott).
12. The life of Christ. Search Ministries has developed an evangelistic Bible study designed specifically for home use: *Who Is This Man Jesus?* available from Multnomah Books.

GETTING STARTED

When inviting friends to participate in the study, don't panic. Here is a suggested invitation: "I'm sure you are aware, Bill, of the pressures on the family today. Homes are breaking up at an unprecedented rate. Ruthe and I are concerned about these trends, and we have invited five to six couples to participate in a study of biblical principles of marriage and family life. We'd love to have you join us." Incidentally, I have found marriage and family to be one of the most valuable topics for an evangelistic study. Chuck Swindoll's book, *Strike the Original Match,* is an excellent text to use. It has a study guide which makes it even more valuable.

If the study is going to focus on one of the books of the Bible, an invitation might sound something like this:"I know you are aware that for years the Bible has been the number one selling book in the world. No man is really educated who is not at least familiar with its basic content. We thought it would be fun to get seven to eight couples together and work through selected portions of John's Gospel. The study will be informal and discussion-centered. We'd love to have you join us." After the initial introduction, you should discuss the length of the series. People are more apt to come if they know it is for only eight to ten weeks.

A series of videos may be the easiest way to launch a neighborhood study. One church in Texas started twenty-six evangelistic home Bible studies by showing the Moody Science videos each week for twelve weeks. Your church could rent one video per week and schedule it to be shown in a different neighborhood each night during the week. When the video series is over, most of the groups will want to continue. They have made new friends, they have been challenged intellectually and spiritually, and have tasted fellowship at a deeper level. Of course, being perceptive, you have anticipated this response and are ready to suggest that the group take another ten weeks to study John's Gospel (or Romans or marriage and family).

Believe that people will find Christ. Expect them to respond and anticipate sharing Christ personally. Look for opportunities to talk individually with seeking people in or out of your study. I find it best to set up an appointment where we can discuss their concerns in private with no fear of interruption.

Make your home circle an open circle whether or not you have a formal study. Believe me, if your non-Christian acquaintances become your friends, they already are predisposed to become a friend of Christ. Isn't that what evangelism is all about —living beautifully and opening up our webs of relationships so that others can see Christ's beauty in us?

Notes

1. Leighton Ford, *The Christian Persuaders* (New York: Harper & Row, 1966), 70.

2. James Jauncey, *Psychology for Successful Evangelism* (Chicago: Moody Press, 1972), 60.

Your Nonbelieving Neighbor

S o you want to be a neighbor to someone spiritually. You desire to develop the capacity to draw near. How do you do it?

KEYS TO DEVELOPING REDEMPTIVE RELATIONSHIPS

Here are some keys—some simple guidelines or stepping stones—to developing redemptive relationships. You will likely use two or three at the same time to help you become an effective member of the second incarnation.

Visualize the Neighborhood
Readiness for Christ

Visualize the Spirit of God hovering over your neighborhood. This is the first key. When I go fishing, birds are often the key to locating fish. Gulls will frequently circle a spot because feeding fish are driving the small minnows (their dinner) to the surface. Gulls join the feeding frenzy and inadvertently tip off the perceptive fisherman where to fish for his dinner.

The effective evangelist believes God's Spirit will lead him to the schooling fish. No one wants to be involved in a losing proposition. Many budding fishers of men are defeated before they get a line in the water because they are convinced no one is interested, seeking, or prepared by God. Our Lord has already told us the fields are ripe for harvest. Believe me there are Spirit-prepared people living near you who are seeking answers. God will lead you to these people like the birds lead fishermen to fish—if you're looking.

For many, the first step in neighborhood evangelism is attitudinal. If they think they will be successful or unsuccessful, they will. What we anticipate in life is usually what we get. If you believe you can't do it, you're probably right. But God says you can. Who do you intend to believe? Actually, this is a very practical principle which shapes your whole attitude and approach to being a neighbor.

I'm a jogger, and as I run through my neighborhood, I see more than just houses, garages, and automobiles. Those houses have people with names and faces living in them. Those I know by name I remember by name. As I regularly visualize the Spirit of God hovering over my neighborhood, I am encouraged to be about the King's business. Obviously, not every neighbor is ready or responsive, but remember the pattern. Witness begins with *cultivation,* moves to *sowing,* and then on to *reaping.* For some, the extent of your evangelistic mission may be to simply expose them to a healthy presence — the music of the gospel. I hope God will use you to bring others of your neighbors to the point of an explanation of the good news (the words of the gospel). The last chapter will focus on how to present the words.

When you have cultivated a friendship and become aware of some of your friend's needs, your gospel presentation becomes much more powerful, a potential solution to both his real and felt needs. When a friendship has been established, it is much easier to sense the appropriate time for moving from cultivation to sowing and reaping. Often our attempts to reap are premature because we don't know the person's spiritual condition.

Make an Initial Acquaintance

God knows the responsive hearts in your sphere of influence. How do you locate them? Social relationships are the key to finding the Spirit-prepared, schooling fish.

This, then, is the second key: *Those who respond to you socially are the schooling fish.* To carry the fishing analogy (not without biblical precedent) a step further, your divine fish locator is social relationships. As you begin to relate to your neighbors, some will respond to you and some won't. Again, it is important that you seek the Lord's help in building genuine friendships. It shouldn't be a relationship with a hook. Those who respond to you are great candidates for discovering Christ.

I have seen this principle affirmed over and over again. One day I spent forty-five minutes with a neighbor discussing the essence of the gospel. He initiated the conversation, and as we sat watching the surf at the Oregon coast, I shared some foundational principles of the gospel. The conversation was both casual and deeply significant. This moment came after months of friendship. Both families spent the morning together playing on the beach. We consider them good friends; we enjoy their company. After talking about spiritual things, we shifted the conversation to the possibility of some fishing trips in the fall.

A real estate firm in Salem, Oregon, assigns each of its agents a five-hundred family "farm." The agents are expected to contact every family once a month for a year. The contact may be a personal one, a telephone call, or a letter. Research indicates that it takes at least six contacts for people to remember who the agent is and whom he represents. During this time of building relationships, the agents are encouraged *not* to go in the house (good psychology, everyone else is trying to get his foot in the door). Furthermore, they are encouraged *not* to ask for a listing. There are exceptions to these restrictions, but they illustrate what it takes to create a favorable climate for selling real estate. After the initial year of regular contacts, the agent continues to communicate with his "farm members" on a scheduled, systematic basis. If this pattern is followed consistently for a year and a half, the agent will get 80 percent of the listings.

What do they know that we either don't know or overlook?

First, people do not like to be confronted by strangers seeking entrance into their homes. The salesman at the door is automatically confronted with a high sales resistance. If the door is opened, the homemaker does it with a determination not to be taken in by sales talk. However, if a friend comes over and shares a glowing testimony of the value of the salesman's product, the reaction is apt to be markedly different. A satisfied customer is the most effective salesperson.

Second, people are more inclined to do business with acquaintances than strangers. It takes time and effort to build a healthy decision-making climate. Third, there is no substitute for time. Sometimes it is necessary to make haste slowly.

Your goal is to build a climate for effective decision making. We lived at our present location for over two years before we began to see people respond. With great anticipation we wait for the harvest. We are surrounded by schooling fish. So are you.

You cannot adopt a five-hundred family farm, but how about a five to ten family farm? By extending your friendship to the neighborhood at large, you will discover three to four families who seem responsive. Block parties, Christmas open houses, and other neighborhood activities provide opportunities for exposure.

Establish a Growing Relationship

A third key follows close on the heels of the second: *To discover schooling fish, you must get acquainted.* Ask God to help you get to know your neighbors. Learn their names and be certain you pronounce them correctly. Smile! Be the kind of family your neighbors would want to know. If you want to build redemptive friendships, be friendly. Be a good listener. Discover and discuss your neighbor's interests rather than your own. Many Christians get tongue-tied when it comes to conversation with non-Christians. Sometimes it's helpful if you have some subjects in mind, such as:

> Profession or career
> Hobbies
> Sports and recreation
> Family activities and interests
> Vacations
> Children's activities and accomplishments
> Current news items
> Personal properties (boat, cars, pets, gardens)
> Religious background

Current projects and home improvements
Current books and films

Take the initiative to be of help when it is appropriate. If he's painting his house, grab a brush! Offer to mow the lawn and look after the house and pets while they're on vacation. Do they need a baby-sitter? Sit for them. Take their children on a picnic with yours.

Extend an Invitation to Your Home

A fourth key is *to invite them to your home.* Your goal is to advance your backyard-fence relationship toward a more significant friendship. Meals are a great way to do it. As a general rule, it is good to have a definite reason for inviting them. It may be simply to enjoy your new barbecue recipe or share some homemade ice cream. They might enjoy seeing slides of your vacation trip (notice I said "might"). Don't be too elaborate if you entertain them for dinner. A formal dinner with crystal, china, and sterling silver isn't necessary. They would probably feel more relaxed and at home with a good barbecued hamburger and a Coke. If your meal is too elaborate you are less likely to be invited to their home because the wife may not be able to match your production. This does not mean the meal cannot be prepared and served in a lovely, gracious manner. It should be!

But what if you feel awkward about entertaining non-Christians? You feel socially inept? Find someone in your church who has the gift of hospitality and invite them and your neighbor over for dinner. Explain your dilemma to them and let them help you ease through. Blend their gift with your concern and you've got a winning combination. Their warmth and social skills can be the catalyst to weld the bond of friendship between you and your neighbor. Believe me, it works!

Sometimes as a gesture of friendship, your neighbor may bring over a bottle of wine. This is a common and accepted social grace in the non-Christian community. Don't panic. A judging, self-righteous attitude is not necessary (or biblical). You have three options. First, if you are not free before the Lord to participate (as with any doubtful thing), you may thank them for their thoughtfulness and graciously decline, returning it to them. Second, you can graciously decline but offer to serve them. Many feel free before the Lord to do this. Third, if your conscience has liberty in this area, you may thank them and participate if you desire. Whatever else may be said, the sin is not participation (assuming freedom of conscience); it is intoxication. Within the Christian community around the world, I have observed mature, Spirit-led, knowledgeable Christians exercise each of the options. Regardless of your personal position, if you are going to be with non-Christians, be prepared to respond to this type of situation in a loving, sensitive manner.

When your neighbors are over for dinner, don't feel compelled to say something spiritual. Many seem to feel that if they have not shared their witness before the evening is over, they have failed. Not so. One couple we saw trust Christ took three years of careful cultivation. For most of that period, spiritual things were off limits; we were not free to discuss such matters. During this time we probably ate together at least thirty times. I wish you could meet this couple today! Patience does pay off.

I suggest that you have grace at the meal. It is your home and it is natural for you to do this. Don't preach or share a quickie witness during the prayer. Be brief and thank the Lord for your neighbors by name. I usually do not lead in prayer when we are at a restaurant with non-Christians. This can be embarrassing for them.

Cultivate Common Interests

A fifth key is *do things together.* The goal is to build a reservoir of common, shared experiences. As your backyard-fence relationship develops, discover what interests them. Sometimes it's good to think through a list of possible common ground contact points. Put a check by those that would be options for you as you think about specific neighbors and their interests.

Tennis	Hunting	Service clubs
Golf	Skiing	Garden clubs
Fishing	Cycling	Coffee

Sewing	Jogging	Flying
Boating	Scouting	Gardening
Model trains	P.T.A.	Woodworking
Bowling	Investments	Playing bridge
Racquetball	Sports events	Cooking classes
Movies	Rodeos	Gourmet clubs
Concerts	Lunch	Guns
Stitchery	Ice skating	Eating
Quiltmaking	Rafting	Knitting
Hiking	Recreational vehicles	Volunteer activities

Certainly there are items in this list both you and your neighbor enjoy in common. Discover these contact points and use them as relational building blocks. You probably have a number of common interests. As I sit here in my study writing, my wife is with a neighbor lady going through some model homes. They both share an interest in interior design.

When you are in your neighbor's home, look for clues to his or her interests. A shop full of woodworking tools, a well-stocked sewing room, or basement shelves full of home-canned fruits can be excellent contact points. Seasonal events such as fairs, rodeos, and ball games are built-in opportunities for friendship cultivation.

Twice Ruthe and I have organized block parties which involved as many as seventy-five people. The police were quite willing to block off the street for us. This done, we borrowed tables and chairs from the church and set them up for serving and eating. Volleyball nets strung across the street provided an outlet for the athletically inclined. Contests and prizes for the kids—bike decorating, egg tossing, sack races—proved to be popular. Six barbecues were rounded up for cooking hamburgers. Cranking the homemade ice cream freezer added to the fun.

Block parties are super for providing a quick exposure to your "family farm." It enables you to look for responsive people who may be candidates for the good news. If for no other reason, these parties are worth doing just for the fun and fellowship.

Make Holidays Count

Capitalize on the holiday seasons. Christmas, New Years, Labor Day, and Thanksgiving provide great opportunities for extending and enriching relationships within your family farm. Why not plan the greatest Christmas open house on your block! Pack them in, serve some super refreshments, sing carols together, and then let different neighbors recount the most memorable events of past Christmases. There is no need for a devotional or gospel witness to make the evening a success. Last Christmas we went to a neighborhood caroling party with about fifty neighbors. In the fall we borrowed a cider press and invited some neighbors over to make cider and eat doughnuts.

Be sensitive to widows, widowers, one-parent families, and those who are alone during the holidays. Since moving to Portland, we've had the joy of sharing our holiday season with an elderly widower. He doesn't yet know the Lord, but our family prays for him and believes God is going to touch his heart. The last time I took him to lunch, I got him talking about the old steam-driven threshing machines of another era. As he answered my dozens of questions, he lit up and glowed. He knew all about how they worked, and it brought back happy memories to relive some of his childhood years. I was thoroughly fascinated. When we last had him over for dinner, he held me and my son Stephen spellbound for nearly an hour as he talked about his experiences working in mines. Soon I intend to share the simple plan of salvation. We believe he has heard the music of the gospel as he shared our hearth and home on numerous occasions. We love him and believe that he knows it.

Capitalize on holidays. They're great times to show your love in special ways. Hearts are often more receptive during these special times of the year.

Be Available for the Hurting

A seventh key is more urgent: *Be available to help when people hurt.* Life is tough. Sickness, death of a loved one, marital problems, financial reversals, and other pressures provide opportunities for the Christian to express Christ's love through serving and caring for members of his farm family. Remember, people don't care how much (or what) you know until they know how much you care! The hurts of others are your opportunities to become good news to them. I believe those opportunities are often arranged by God himself. A helping hand and a sympathetic, listening spirit give your beliefs validity and impact. Mowing lawns, taking over meals, baby-sitting, shopping, and driving are some ways to help people in need.

One caution: Don't forget…you have needs. How about letting others meet some of them? Maybe the greatest gift you can share is the gift of your need. When conversations focus on some of the normal marriage and family problems, remember that you have some, too. Don't act as if you don't or you'll come across inauthentic.

In relational evangelism, availability is often the greatest ability. Be a listening, sensitive, giving, caring Christian friend. It's contagious.

Become a Giver of Books

An eighth key is an easy one to adopt: *Give them something to read or listen to.* Be casual about it. Put some good Christian literature on your coffee table. Be sure they are top quality, such as James Dobson's *Love for a Lifetime* or Max Lucado's *No Wonder They Call Him the Savior*. Stick with books that are need-centered and have good graphics. Often your guest will pick up a book and start thumbing through it. If he expresses an interest, give it to him or drop by later with another. Have some on hand that you can give away. "Hey, Bill, this is a super book. I'd love for you to read it and tell me what you think of it."

If your non-Christian friend is struggling with family concerns, there are many good, helpful books available. If he has a philosophical bent, C. S. Lewis's *Mere Christianity* is a good choice. Check with your local Christian bookstore for other selections suitable for a non-Christian. Whatever you do, be sure they are good quality books. Don't be cheap! Sometimes a modern translation New Testament makes a good gift.

There are some challenging tape series which are effective in evangelism. Be sure, however, that you listen to the tape first! It should be positive in tone and attitude (after all, the gospel is *good news)*, need-centered, and biblically sound. A good evangelistic tape doesn't necessarily have to deal with evangelism. Tapes on marriage and family relations, prophecy, Christian evidences (apologetics), and well-presented personal testimonies can be powerful evangelistic tools. And don't forget music tapes.

Christian magazines should not be overlooked. Parents struggling with teen-agers might be delighted to know about *Campus Life* magazine. *Moody Monthly, World, Marriage Partnership,* and *Virtue* are but a few of the fine magazines available. Often a good way to expose your friend to the gospel is to call attention to an article and then give her the magazine. I generally avoid the bumper sticker, wall plaque mentality, but if you find them useful, at least be sure they are tasteful, accurate, and of good quality.

Be creative in your use of Christian resources. Purchase a supply of quality items and keep them readily available. Consider such expenditures part of your tithe (even if you don't get a tax receipt). Remember, it was God who said that "he who wins souls is wise." In all of these activities, your goal is to become a servant to your neighbor.

Find an Appropriate Harvest Vehicle

A ninth key: *Look for an appropriate harvest vehicle.* Whether you use a lure, a worm, a hook, or a net, fish can be caught in numerous ways. But you have to select the proper bait. You don't use trout flies for yellow tail. Live squid get their attention and make excellent bait.

Once while fishing in Mexican waters for yellow tail, we hit a school of them and boated 131 in a little over an hour. We were using live squid, but that wasn't all that kept the fish coming back. As soon as we hooked up, the deck hands started chumming the water with chopped minnows. In a real sense, we "chum" the spiritual waters as we function as salt and light. In a practical sense we do this by spending time with our non-Christian friends, discovering their interests, sharing their fellowship, and bearing their concerns. But a time comes when it is appropriate to pray toward involving them in some type of harvest vehicle. A sensitivity toward their preferences and views is important. For a nonathletic vegetarian, an invitation to hear an all-pro athlete at a steak fry is not appropriate. If there must be an offense, let it be the offense of the gospel, not the manner in which the gospel is presented.

There are numerous harvest vehicles. Here are some examples:

Evangelistic dinners
Home Bible studies
Businessmen's breakfasts
Mayor's prayer breakfasts
Christian movies
Conferences or retreats
Seminars
Fishing/hunting trips
Church sports programs
Special concerts
Church-sponsored craft classes
Church-sponsored neighborhood teas
Boys Brigade/Indian Guides

The list is limited only by one's creativity. Skim the list again and note how many of these activities are suitable for blending Christians and non-Christians together. Imagine what could happen if a church member with oil painting ability was asked to teach a class open to the general public. A well-equipped shop could be another vehicle for bringing people together in redemptive relationships. A fishing club led by a mature Christian who knows fishing inside and out would be an attractive vehicle to involve your neighbor in if he loves fishing. I've been part of such groups. There is lots of time for getting close to needy people on a fishing trip!

Mariners Church in Newport Beach, California, started because a group of businessmen became burdened for their community. With no intention of planting a church, they started a Christian Leadership Week. The Junior Chamber of Commerce sponsors it. No clergy are involved in its planning or execution; it is totally lay-led and has been very effective.

Each morning businessmen's breakfasts are held in several country clubs in the area. No ministers are allowed to speak. (This keeps it a city-wide event, free from the pressures of the local council of churches.) Two local business people speak at each breakfast. The messages are short and to the point. Speakers are asked to avoid references to specific churches, creeds, or controversial religious issues. The central topic is the gospel and how it has affected them personally. The women sponsor teas and share their testimonies. Evenings are filled with home meetings at which laymen share.

A Mayor's Prayer Breakfast climaxes the week. As many as two thousand attend this function. The same morning, five hundred to six hundred high schoolers pack out a similar breakfast designed just for them. Usually a well-known athlete or public figure speaks at this gathering. Dozens are influenced each year by Christian Leadership Week, a strategic event that provides an opportunity for Christians to invite their non-Christian friends.

A church that takes evangelism seriously should schedule several yearly events, classes, or activities which are appropriate harvest vehicles. These provide opportunities for non-Christians, who may be reluctant to attend a Sunday morning church service, to be exposed to the gospel. You may need to invite your neighbor to three or four harvest vehicles to bring him to a point of decision. Some vehicles are obviously more direct in their presentation of the gospel than others. The cumulative impact is what is important. (Of course some neighbors may come to Christ without involvement in any type of harvest vehicle.) My wife and I found evangelistic Bible studies like those described in the previous chapter to be an especially effective vehicle.

Plant Seeds for Salvation

Your friendship may progress to the point where nonbelieving friends virtually ask you how to become a Christian. This is not uncommon, especially if you have *been a good seed planter*, which is the tenth key. There will be opportunities during your friendship to communicate bits and pieces of both the gospel itself and your own personal testimony. (We already discussed the role of books and tapes in this pre-evangelism process.) The temptation is to unload the entire evangelistic dump truck the first time the conversation turns to spiritual things. As a general rule, this is not a healthy pattern to follow. Gradually directing a person to Christ through seed planting is a much preferred approach.

First, discuss his religious background. "Jim, we've never had a chance to chat about your own religious background. At what point are you in your own spiritual pilgrimage?" (See "The Pilgrimage Question" section in chapter 11.) Don't ask if he is a Christian. Often he will say "yes" and yet not have any understanding of the new birth. It then becomes necessary to prove that his affirmation (his "yes") was wrong.

Second, as he discusses his religious background, listen carefully and patiently. Listen for understanding. When the opportunity comes to lead him to Christ, it is helpful to know something of his background, beliefs, and experiences. By listening selectively, the evangelist notes key words which reveal the person's objectives, needs, fears, and problems.

Listen for permission to continue the discussion. As you interact, note carefully his response. Although he may not ask you to stop the conversation, by listening perceptively, you can often tell when the conversation strays outside his comfort zone. Time and trust are the two keys to gradually stretching his comfort zone. Insensitivity at this point may close the door to any further discussion. Stretch him, yes, but not to the breaking point. Watch for signs of nervousness, wandering attention, a change of subject, or nonverbal evidences of hostility and resentment.

Third, eliminate caricatures of the gospel. This is one of the most important dimensions of seed planting. As the non-Christian contemplates the vast puzzle of Christianity, he visualizes a lot more pieces in it than Christ and the cross. Let me list a few of these distortions.

1. "Christianity is keeping the golden rule. Therefore, for me to become a Christian, I must try harder." Hardly good news to someone who has tried and tried and failed and failed. To eliminate this caricature of the gospel, plant this thought. Just the other day my neighbor said to me, "I'm not a very religious person." I replied, "I'm not either. I was delighted to discover that Christianity isn't a religion, it's a relationship with a person, Jesus Christ." That to most non-Christians is a revolutionary idea. If you do nothing more than eliminate that caricature, you will have made great progress in your evangelistic enterprise. It may be appropriate to stop the conversation at that point without pursuing it further. Believe me, the non-Christian who comes to understand just this one point has something to go home and think about. If you're his friend, he will!

2. *"To become a Christian I must give up everything that I enjoy."* This is a partial truth. His observations have led him to conclude that Christians never have any fun. The caricature could be stated this way: "Christians are negative people. I don't want to be so negative; therefore, I don't want to be a Christian." Unfortunately, some Christians act in ways which reinforce the caricature. A super time at the beach can bury this caricature in a hurry—assuming you invite them along. You can be the key to eliminating this distortion.

3. *"To become a Christian I must go to church and get involved in lots of meetings."* This is the old "churchianity" caricature. Unfortunately, some of our churches perpetuate this idea by pushing a program which encourages a neurotic Christian activism. I told my neighbor I wasn't interested in lots of meetings, but that I did enjoy regular times of *significant* teaching and worship.

Obviously, the list of caricatures could go on and on. Take a pencil and paper and list a few of your own.

Caricatures are reasons for rejecting the gospel. As you plant seeds which gradually eliminate caricatures, you move your neighbor closer and closer to the cross. There are usually many "predecisions" which precede *the* decision. Elimination of caricatures predisposes the non-Christian toward making *the* decision. Each time the non-Christian has a caricature challenged, he faces a decision point. To reject a caricature is to remove one more excuse.

If he discovers "Christians have more fun," he can no longer use the "no fun" caricature as an excuse. If he decides to reject the caricature, he has unknowingly taken a step toward the acceptance of Christ. The pre-decision decision has been made, and the nonbeliever moves one step closer to the cross. Believers must be very sensitive to the distortions of Christianity which exist in the nonbeliever's mind. Our behavior either reinforces or removes these caricatures. Be a remover, not a reinforcer!

The fourth step to take as a seed planter is to highlight the positive aspects of the gospel. This you can do verbally and nonverbally. It involves all that we have said about how knowing Christ affects various aspects of everyday life. "My wife and I have found that knowing Christ is a major key to our relationship as husband and wife." "Knowing Christ has given me a great peace of heart." "It's a wonderful thing to know that God has forgiven me for all my failures." Spread over time, perceptive seed planting bears great fruit. It eventually leads you to the point of sharing the words of the gospel.

Be Ready to Share

The final key: *Be prepared to set the hook.* We do need to be able to share the *words* of the gospel. What a joy it is to introduce your friends to a saving knowledge of Jesus Christ. We will discuss how to personally share Christ in the final chapter.

CHAPTER 11

Your Personal Message of Evangelism

*I*t's time to share the words of the gospel. At this point, Christians are known to panic. They know the world's greatest, the world's most important, the world's most life-changing secret. And when its time to tell, they choke. As ambassadors for Christ, they have the privilege of delivering the best news that any individual could possibly receive. You would think that sharing the good news would be one of life's most fulfilling and sought after experiences. In reality, it's the one thing most Christians fear and avoid at all costs.

There are numerous reasons for such a response. Let me suggest two. Many Christians don't know *how* to share their faith. They have never disciplined themselves to learn a logical, biblical gospel presentation. A second hindrance is that many times the Christian doesn't know the person he is evangelizing. As a result, the witnessing experience is often an embarrassment to both parties.

I have shared Christ on numerous occasions with virtual strangers and have seen some of them respond. Praise the Lord for those who trust Christ under such circumstances! Unfortunately, only a small percentage of people become believers through such an encounter. Our goal is to mobilize the *majority* of believers to be involved in evangelism as a way of life. Natural evangelism provides the most satisfying option for the largest number of believers. As a general rule, it is easier to share with a friend. And what a joyous occasion it proves to be. I often find tears of joy coursing down my cheeks as another friend trusts Christ.

When have we come to the point in a relationship where it is appropriate to present the gospel and call for a decision? And what should we say when we do reach that point?

DETERMINING READINESS FOR THE GOSPEL

How do you know when you have reached this decision point? Let me answer this question by asking you some questions.

1. What do you know of the person's religious background?

2. What opportunities have you had to plant seeds? What was the response to these germinal ideas?

3. Do you sense that your neighbor enjoys being with you?

4. What needs have you discovered that the gospel provides the solution for?

5. What caricatures have you been able to eliminate from his arsenal of questions and excuses?

6. What signs of openness have you detected?

    a. questions about religious things

    b. general freedom to discuss religious concepts

    c. openness to reading materials and other resources

    d. willing involvement in some harvest vehicles

    e. positive seeking attitude

7. How much of your personal testimony have you had a chance to share?

These questions are simply aids to help you decide whether the appropriate time has come. It is important that you be sensitive about timing. A familiar pledge among salesmen is illustrative: "I will not begin talking about my solution until I'm certain my prospect is eager to hear about it." Remember, the Spirit of God convicts men of sin, righteousness, and judgment. The effective evangelist is in a cooperative relationship with God himself. To be insensitive to or to fail to wait for evidences of the moving of the Spirit in the unbeliever's life is to hinder God's work.

KNOWING WHAT TO SAY

Let's assume that you feel your friend is getting close to a salvation decision point. You know something of his background, his needs, and the caricatures he embraces. What's next? Generally it is time to ask some key questions which test the water.

The Pilgrimage Question

There is no magic question, but I've found this one helpful. I call it my *pilgrimage question:* "Bill, we've never had a chance to talk about your own religious background. At what point are you in your own spiritual pilgrimage?"

Notice that this question acknowledges that coming to God involves a normal (but supernatural) process. Thus the individual feels that it is okay to still be in process. The pilgrimage question does not ask whether one is a Christian or not. If asked that question, most people will say "yes" because they don't really understand what being a Christian is all about. Then your task becomes one of proving their "yes" answer to be wrong.

The pilgrimage question is general enough to allow a response without embarrassment. No one likes to be put on the spot. This question allows a person to choose a response appropriate to his own theological comfort zone. His answer can be as simple or profound as he desires it to be.

The chief advantage of the pilgrimage question is that it gives you one final time for spiritual appraisal. As you listen carefully to the response, you make the final decision as to whether or not to share the gospel of saving grace at this time.

Allowing a person to talk about his pilgrimage gives you a subtle advantage. It predisposes him to listen to you at the appropriate time. When you are ready to share the gospel, you want to do most of the talking. Let him talk first. Resist the temptation to jump into the conversation and deal with side issues. If he believes his church is the only true church offering the only true baptism producing the only true believers, don't debate. Just listen! Affirm the truth of his *valid* insights, because you will soon have to challenge his viewpoint in some critical areas.

A related question is also helpful: "Has your spiritual pilgrimage come to the point of a personal commitment to Jesus Christ, or are you still on the way?" When people start talking about the state of their spiritual pilgrimage you soon have all the information needed for the next step. I've had many respond to this question by saying, "I'm still on the way." Great! If that's their response, I'll usually say, "Well, Bill, maybe the next step God has for you is coming to understand how to establish a personal, saving relationship with him."

Opportunity Statement

Because the purpose of the pilgrimage question is to give non-believers the opportunity to pour out their religious beliefs, feelings, and concerns first, I usually find that little time is left for me to talk. Consequently, I plant seeds to prepare for a later discussion. I find it helpful to move from the pilgrimage question to this *opportunity statement:* "Sometime I'd like the opportunity to share four principles that will help you to understand what it means to have a personal relationship with Christ." A little later in the conversation I might reinforce this by saying, "Bill, I can understand your rejection of religion, with all its formality and hypocrisy. When I get an opportunity to share those principles with you, they should help answer your questions."

In some conversations I have dropped the idea of a further discussion five or six times. The response to this repeated suggestion must be observed and properly interpreted. It becomes your red or green light. You may be thinking that such an approach is devious, humanistic, and unnecessary. On the contrary, the Bible teaches we are not to throw pearls to swine. Interpreted, the Lord is saying among other things that audience awareness is very important. He refused to perform miracles when he sensed hearts were hard. Sensitivity is what we are talking about. It is part of being "wise as serpents."

You can always count on this: As you discuss spiritual things, all the powers of hell will go into operation to thwart your efforts. It is imperative that we be well-prepared, sharp instruments the Spirit can use effectively and decisively. I am not suggesting a rote, mechanistic way of dealing with people. These are general principles which are to be adapted to specific, changing situations. No pilgrimage to God will involve all of these elements.

Interest Question

As the initial discussion time closes, it is often helpful to change the opportunity statement into a question.

> *Pilgrimage Question:* At what point are you in your spiritual pilgrimage?
>
> *Opportunity Statement:* Sometime I'd like the opportunity to share four principles that will help you to understand what it means to have a personal relationship with Christ.
>
> *Interest Question:* Could I share those four principles with you?

This polite offer now allows your listener to talk. It is his turn to respond.

Schedule Question

If the response is positive to the interest question ("Yes, I'd appreciate your sharing them," or "Sounds great"), schedule becomes the next focal point. Do you share the principles now or later? If later, some scheduling questions are important. "What's the best time for us to get together?" "Is morning okay for you?" "Is Wednesday or Friday better for you?" "How about coming by my office (home) and we can talk about this some more?" Once a time is agreed upon…rejoice! Harvest is scheduled. A schooling fish has been identified, cultivated, and is about to take life's most important step! A new birth, a beginning *as new* as birth itself, is about to take place.

Gospel Explanation

With a scheduled time and place, the next step is the *gospel explanation.* At this point the gospel itself (those four principles or whatever explanation of the gospel you prefer) is explained. The last section of this chapter describes how to summarize and present the gospel.

Decision Questions

Once the gospel has been clearly set forth, the *decision questions* are the next logical step. Here we are simply asking the individual to personalize the truth. I usually find the following three questions to be helpful:

1. Does this (the gospel) make sense to you?
2. On the basis of this (the gospel presentation) have you ever committed your life to Jesus Christ as your Savior?
3. Is there any reason why you wouldn't want to trust Christ right now?

Your friend is now at the point of decision. If he responds positively to the Spirit's wooing, he by faith will become a new creature in Christ.

The *pilgrimage question* is a spiritual litmus test. The *opportunity statement* is seed planting at its best (never underestimate the power of suggestion). It rouses curiosity and suggests a future course of action, a potential solution to some personal problems. The *interest question* is your way of determining whether your friend is open to and interested in pursuing conversation about the gospel. Assuming he is, the *schedule question* puts a definite time frame into the decision making process. "Sometime" becomes next Tuesday at 8:00 A.M. Then comes the *gospel explanation,* the *decision questions,* and the commitment to Christ!

Obviously, at any point in this communication sequence, the response could be negative. Your friend may express an interest in hearing those mysterious four principles, but be hesitant when you start talking schedule. Don't panic. Praise God he's expressed a positive response to the idea of discussing spiritual things. Back off, continue to be his friend, and wait for another opportunity. I actually had a neighbor call me up and say, almost in desperation, "Joe, you've *got* to share those principles with me." I did. He's now a brother in Christ.

The following chart helps us see what options we might pursue at each stage of the communication sequence based on our non-Christian friend's responses.

- **Continuous Cultivation of a Growing, Deepening Relationship**

- **Pilgrimage Question:** "At what point are you ... ?"
  POSITIVE RESPONSE   NEUTRAL/NEGATIVE RESPONSE

- **Opportunity Statement:** "Sometime I'd like the opportunity..."
  POSITIVE RESPONSE   NEUTRAL/NEGATIVE RESPONSE

- **Interest Question:** "Could I share those 4 principles with you?"
  POSITIVE RESPONSE   NEUTRAL/NEGATIVE RESPONSE

- **Schedule Question:** "What would be a good time for you?"
  POSITIVE RESPONSE   NEUTRAL/NEGATIVE RESPONSE

- **Opportunity Explanation:** Share the 4 principles.
  POSITIVE RESPONSE   NEUTRAL/NEGATIVE RESPONSE

- **Decision Questions:** "Is there any reason why you wouldn't receive Christ right now?
  POSITIVE RESPONSE   NEUTRAL/NEGATIVE RESPONSE

- **The Decision:** Accept Christ

- **Assurance and Follow-up**

Back off and continue developing the relationship

As a person approaches a decision for Christ, a major key is confidence. Believe, indeed *expect*, the individual will trust the Lord. You've seen him at work in your friend's life as you've spent time together. It's time to anticipate the rejoicing of angels in heaven! Fully expect God to bring the person to a point of salvation.

So what do you do before your scheduled appointment? Begin by praying a lot. Although God uses human agency, it is God who draws people to himself. But don't forget...you are important to the process.

Then, if you haven't learned a good, logical gospel presentation, by all means learn one. You may be saying, "I don't like methods. I prefer to just trust the Spirit of God." The fallacy of this reasoning is that "no method" is a method. It's the "no method" method. It's the "hamburger in the fan" approach to effective communication. Certainly we do not harness the creative Holy Spirit with assembly line methodology. But the logical organization of the gospel essentials does not have to rule out creativity and diversity in presentation and emphasis.

I have presented the four spiritual principles hundreds of times, and I'm sure the presentation has varied in emphasis and content each time. My desire is to adapt my presentation to the needs of the person I am sharing with. Granted, the great diversity of personalities calls for a diversity in the way we approach people with the gospel. This fact, however, in no way rules out a carefully planned methodology.

The Holy Spirit puts no premium on lack of preparation or shoddy thinking. The Creator has designed our thinking process to follow rational patterns of communication to logical conclusions. A disorganized, haphazard gospel presentation violates both natural and spiritual laws. Whatever else may be said, God is not the author of confusion. On the other hand, logic, brilliance, or the powers of persuasion are not to be a substitute for the Spirit. A carefully thought through presentation communicates to the listener that the message is important and worthy of his attention. Here are some characteristics of a good method:

1. Biblically accurate and balanced
2. Logical in its development with good transitions between its major points
3. Clear in its content, avoiding churchy, unfamiliar language
4. Clear in its intent, with no question about the action steps necessary for the individual to receive Christ

5. Positive in its basic content, reflecting the reality that the gospel is good news

6. Simple rather than complex

7. Attractively designed, quality piece of literature (if printed).

PRINCIPLES FOR A PERSONAL GOSPEL PRESENTATION

Before looking at the actual sharing process, let's consider some foundational communication principles.

In sharing the gospel, we are actually *converting biblical facts into people benefits.* Jesus did not come to condemn the world. Keep this in mind as you share the good news. Justification, translated into modern terminology, offers incredible people benefits. Besides being God's provision to deliver me from judgment, it is the key to deliverance from guilt with all its interpersonal ramifications. The indwelling Christ is the answer to the powerlessness and futility of the nonbeliever's everyday existence. Highlight these benefits.

The effective evangelist works toward *establishing a supportive, nourishing climate for communication.* Only 7 percent of effective communication is verbal, 38 percent is tone of voice, and 55 percent is totally nonverbal. If you establish a defensive environment, the unbeliever will spend most of his time trying to guard himself against both you and your message. Eliminate your holy hush, stained-glass voice, or your sanctimonious twang. You are not a judge or a jury either. You are a sinner showing another sinner how to draw water from the well of life. A caring, sensitive manner is vital for sharing the good news. If you view this as a contest between you and the prospective believer, it will be reflected in your attitude, tone, and behavior. The unbeliever is not an enemy and the evangelist must not seek a decision in a battleground mindset. If victory at all costs is what we value, this attitude will vitally influence the way we relate to others. The goal is to win friends, not arguments. Sharing Christ is not something we do to an unbeliever as an object; it is something we do with an unbeliever as his friend, confidant, and guide.

The effective evangelist *communicates empathy by asking questions and listening carefully.* Empathy is the ability to become a naturalized citizen of another person's world. The effective evangelist uses empathy to help discover the unbeliever's problems and devise gospel solutions. Generally, people are not afraid to believe, but they are afraid of being "sold." Questions are necessary diagnostic tools because people hear answers only to the questions they are asking. Communication is not complete until the recipient hears with understanding. Our questions not only help us uncover their questions and concerns, but they convey that we care. Well-designed questions help develop tension between what is and what ought to be. Spirit-directed questions can build conviction which in turn moves the unbeliever toward the gospel solution. By listening carefully and using questions skillfully, the evangelist communicates empathy.

I have found that questions are most effective in the early stages of sharing the gospel. They become tools to aid discussion and seek "pilgrimage status" information. As a general rule, the more questions have been used in the early states, the less they are needed when it is appropriate to explain the gospel. Key questions may be asked *months* before the actual gospel presentation. This helps your presentation because the unbeliever has already had his day in court; he has had an opportunity to share his beliefs and voice his opinions. Now it is your turn to talk, and because you have listened and used questions wisely, your gospel presentation has added impact.

Effective communication is marked by humility and gentleness. If you don't know the answer to a question, admit it. Don't assume an "I know everything" attitude. The goal is not to smother the unbeliever with facts. Often we try to communicate too much too fast.

Effective evangelists eliminate everything that is offensive (other than the offense of the cross itself). Bad breath, unkempt clothes, and poor personal hygiene are inexcusable. Lighting, ventilation, and privacy, while not gospel essentials, should not be overlooked. Not to be sensitive to the unbeliever's schedule is also wrong. Be on time and finish at the appropriate time.

Let's assume you are with your friend and are ready to move from the normal small talk to spiritual things. How do you do it? The following suggestions are just that—suggestions. You will have to develop a gospel presentation which is comfortable to you.

A Transition

The first challenge you face is to change the conversation to spiritual things. A good transition is the key. Campus Crusade for Christ has one I use often. "Just as there are physical laws which govern the universe, there are spiritual laws which govern our relationship with God. Bill, I'd like to share four of these principles with you." I often explain that whether or not I believe in the law of gravity, if I jump off a building, I'll become a believer. Recognition doesn't determine reality. Whether I recognize it or not, our universe is controlled by physical and spiritual laws. My denial of these facts does not change the reality of them.

Paper and Pencil

I prefer to actually write out the four laws (basics of the gospel) on a piece of paper. There are many advantages to this. First, it is more personal than reading from a booklet. Second, it focuses attention on what you are doing. Third, it enables you to personalize your presentation. You can add diagrams or illustrations. Fourth, you can give the sheet to them when you're finished. If you don't, most people will ask you for it. It becomes a precious document, a sort of birth certificate for many of them. I've had people open their Bibles and show me their "certificate" years after I shared Christ with them. In a Madison Avenue world with prepackaged everything, it's nice to add a personal touch.

Hold the Questions

This is your time to share. You've allowed your friend to describe his pilgrimage. You've asked questions and listened carefully. If a question comes up now, don't let it interrupt your train of thought with an answer. Instead, compliment your friend and make a suggestion: "Bill, that's a very perceptive question. Would it be okay to hold that question until I've finished sharing the rest of these principles? I believe your question will be answered. If not, I'd be happy to respond to it." A deferred question seldom comes up again when the gospel has been clearly presented. Sometimes it is impossible (and unwise) to defer a question. If that is the case, answer it briefly and move on.

Read or Quote the Pertinent Scripture Verses

The Word is quick and powerful. Use it. If it is possible, let your friend look on with you as you read. It will be a great joy as you experience the Spirit of God using his holy Word to direct people to Jesus Christ. I would guard against using too much Scripture, however. Once you have made your point, move on. Also, use a modern translation your friend can understand.

Plant Seeds Again

Several times during the gospel presentation I like to suggest the appropriate and expected action that needs to be taken. "Bill, *when* you make a commitment to Christ, you will discover what it means to have the peace of God." "*When* you receive Christ you will find that God will help you in your family relationships." "*When* Christ becomes part of your life, the God-shaped vacuum in your life will be filled." This lets your friend know what the appropriate and expected action is. It conveys confidence on your part that he both needs to make this decision and that he will. Our verbal message needs to be backed up by our nonverbal message. If we convey fear, uncertainty, and tentativeness nonverbally, our friend is receiving contradictory messages.

It is reasonable to expect a favorable response. Having cultivated a friendship and bathed it in prayer, what else should we expect? Are the fields ripe or not? When you're standing knee-deep in a field ready for harvest, why be hesitant? Suggesting the action step several times also prepares the person for the coming call to commitment. On numerous occasions the nonbeliever is so prepared by God that I've actually had him ask, "Well, how do I receive him?" before I've finished the presentation.

Another advantage to this "when you" seed planting is that it builds your own confidence. For most Christians the hardest part of sharing the gospel is calling for a commitment. Seed planting makes it easier and less threatening to transition to this vital part of the gospel.

Share Analogous Examples

Analogous examples are "If the shoe fits, wear it" types. Because you know some of your friend's needs, you can use illustrations of others with similar needs who found a solution in Christ. Suppose you have noticed that Bill has difficulty expressing love and affection. Without making reference to his need, you might say, "Bill, a friend of mine whose marriage was in trouble came and told me his concerns. I shared with him that a relationship with Christ could make a significant difference. He received Christ and found that things began to change. He hasn't solved all the problems yet, but he has found renewed hope. When you receive Christ I believe you will be delighted to see the changes he will make in your own life."

Share Personal Experiences

Avoid the old "before Christ I was a revolting rat and now I'm a super saint" mentality. At best, only half of the statement is true. Authenticity is important. Avoid all temptations to pump sunshine. Progress that you have made is appropriate information to share, but don't leave the impression you have arrived. That you are progressing toward a *destination* is good news to many. If they're really friends they've already seen you spill your milk.

Experiences they can identify with are especially valuable. If your friend is struggling with the issue of trusting Christ, describe the fears and apprehensions you had as you approached this decision point (assuming you had them).

Be Natural

I can't stress this enough. Relax. God draws people to himself…through you. Guard against getting too animated. This doesn't mean you need to be impassive and play it cool. Be yourself and talk with (not preach at, manipulate, or coerce) your friend. I am in no way suggesting that you be solemn or sanctimonious. Humor can be very effective as a tension reliever. Use it wisely. Tears? Why not. This is a joyous occasion. I often find myself shedding tears of joy. A prodigal son is coming home. Glory!

Use Repetition and Review for Impact

Regardless of the plan you use, when you have finished one point, review it and move on to the next. "Bill, up to this point, we've seen that God really does love you. You are special to him." When you move on to a third major point, quickly review the other two. This reinforces the truth and increases understanding.

Adapt Your Presentation to His Needs

If because of extreme guilt and insecurity the individual needs reassurance of God's love, spend more time making this point. If he is already broken by sin, don't belabor the issue. The person who knows little about Christ may need you to spend most of your time talking about the uniqueness of the Lord's person and work. For others who understand Christ's uniqueness but have never responded to him, most of your focus should be on their need to receive him as Savior.

Quotations and comments from notable scholars and leaders can make a powerful contribution to your adaptation. Start collecting and memorizing them. I have memorized quotes about Jesus Christ from many notable historical figures. They are especially effective for the individual struggling with the intellectual integrity of a commitment to Christ. Josh McDowell's book, *Evidence that Demands a Verdict,* is full of valuable quotes.

Present the Opportunity to Trust Christ

The time has come to seek a commitment. The *decision questions* described earlier in this chapter provide a helpful way to make this an effective, productive experience.

1. Does this make sense to you?
2. On the basis of this, have you ever committed your life to Jesus Christ as your Savior?
3. Is there any reason why you would not want to trust Christ right now?

The first question helps you know whether or not your friend understands the gospel. The second question provides you with your friend's evaluation of his relationship to Jesus Christ. The third question is particularly important. It does not ask if the person wants to receive Christ, a question that anticipates a yes or no answer. Instead, it asks if there is a *reason* why the unbeliever would not want to trust Christ.

At this point, you anticipate his fear. As you mention praying to receive Christ, many non-Christians panic. They haven't done much praying and fear embarrassment. I've found this to be helpful: "Bill, I've shared Christ with many people, and I've found they sometimes feel awkward praying. I can appreciate that. The words are not important—God knows your heart—but if it makes sense to you, why don't I pray out loud, and if what I pray expresses how you feel, why don't you pray out loud after me? Would that be all right?" If so, I usually lead in prayer, one phrase at a time. Often the individual adds comments of his own. These are precious moments. What a joy to lead your friend to Christ!

Provide Assurance and Follow-up

Most gospel presentations have some simple thoughts to assure the individual of the reality of the new birth. I will not repeat them here. Follow-up is a delight because friends enjoy being together. Again, there are many helpful follow-up books available. Check with your pastor for a suitable one.

Where do you go from here? To the beauty parlor, of course. From there it is out to love a friend to Christ. You'll never have time if I keep writing. I'll quit writing about evangelism so you can start doing it...beautifully. See you in glory. Introduce me to your neighbors when we get there. By God's grace you'll meet some of mine.

A P P E N D I X

B O A R D   E V A L U A T I O N   S H E E T

Growing in Ministry

A. What areas of giftedness do you see being exercised? Romans 12:3-8; 1 Corinthians 12:4-11.

B. What areas of giftedness need to be developed? 1 Timothy 4:14; 2 Timothy 1:6.

C. How has _____ equipped faithful men for ministry during the last year? 2 Timothy 2:2; Ephesians 4:11-16.

D. Are there hindrances to ministry that need to be removed? Hebrews 12:1-2.

Balanced in Priorities

A. How has _____ grown in communion with God? John 15:1-11.

B. How has _____ grown in relationship with his family? Ephesians 5:18-6:4.

C. How has _____ grown in relationship to the body? 1 Corinthians 13:4-7; Ephesians 4:25-32.

D. How has _____ grown in relationship with personal acquaintances? Colossians 4:5-6.

E. How has _____ demonstrated his concern for God's work around the world? Matthew 28:19-20; Acts 1:8.

F. How well does _____'s schedule reflect the biblical priorities of an elder? 1 Timothy 4:7; Romans 12:1-2.

Maturing in Character

A. What qualities of Christ are particularly evident in _____'s life? Galatians 5:22-23; 2 Peter 1:5-9.

B. What qualities of an elder need further development? 1 Timothy 3:1-7; Titus 1:5-9.

C. What project could best stimulate _____'s growth as an elder? Hebrews 10:24-25.

D. Additional comments and suggestions:

Twelve-Session Study Guide

A church in this country, often cited as a model of an evangelizing church, claims nine thousand members. Three hundred members are involved each week in a planned, door-to-door outreach. Since the total membership of the average American church is less than one-third that number, three hundred trained evangelists from one church is amazing . . . until one does a little simple math. Three hundred is less than 4 percent of nine thousand. Praise the Lord for the three hundred, the faithful 4 percent, but what about the 96 percent?

I suspect that most Christians fit into the silent majority—the 96 percent who don't and probably won't! The 96 percent who feel uneasy because they have not rushed out to join the "faithful four."

Life-Style Evangelism was written out of a concern for the lost and a concern for the silent majority, most of whom are concerned, uninvolved, and frustrated. It was also written with an appreciation for the obedience and courage of the "faithful four."

This study guide is designed to walk you through the book and to explore biblical patterns of evangelism (which, by the way, do include the efforts of the "faithful four"). This experience will expand your concept of evangelism and release you to utilize your gifts, abilities, and resources in a redemptive manner. Our goal is to encourage you to become a redemptive person, an ambassador who skillfully represents the King and leverages (in the best sense) the pre-Christian toward the cross.

We must return to basics. The 96 percent cannot remain uninvolved if the Great Commission is to be faithfully implemented. *Life-Style Evangelism* is targeted for Christians functioning within an established church. It presupposes that every believer has webs of relationships (vocational and neighborhood) that he can influence for Christ. It accepts the biblical truth that not everyone reaps, but all are part of a grand scheme of influence and persuasion.

What's in the Guide?

This guide is designed to stimulate interaction with the basic message of the book. It can be used either for individual or group study. The guide contains twelve sessions, each coordinated with the twelve main sections of the book (the introduction plus eleven chapters). Each session has four parts: 1) the purpose of the session, 2) supporting biblical data, 3) thought questions designed to probe and challenge your thinking, and 4) practical ways to implement the truths under consideration.

Where Do You Meet?

A group study can meet anywhere that is conducive to healthy contemplation, discussion, and interaction. If you plan to study on your own, find a quiet corner of your home, office, or classroom. The serious life-style issues addressed in this book warrant careful and prayerful consideration. I recommend the group process if at all possible. Evangelism is ultimately related to and influenced by the corporate life style of the local Christian community, and group discussion is probably the most effective way to stimulate evangelistic effectiveness. The life-style evangelist needs a strong, supportive community that understands and affirms his efforts.

Who Should Be Involved?

The Great Commission was not intended to become the Great Omission. Four percent involvement is not enough. Every believer is called to live redemptively, to cultivate pre-Christian relationships, to use his spiritual gifts for both edification and evangelism. Most need help in developing a balanced, biblical approach to evangelism. Those who have been sidelined by inappropriate methods will profit from this study.

The issues discussed are much broader and go much deeper than a simple discussion of another approach to evangelism. For many this book is a call to radical change of thought and life style. It is a challenge to church leaders to reconsider their philosophy of ministry. Ministers of evangelism will find this study a great tool for motivating the silent majority to become the redemptive majority.

What Is Expected of You?

A careful reading of each session's assigned chapter from *Life-Style Evangelism* is the logical first step. This should be followed by individual interaction with the questions for that chapter. Ideally, the chapter should be read and the questions answered before the group meets. This will enhance discussion and group participation. The group leader should take the responsibility for making the weekly assignments.

The questions become the format for the group meeting. The leader will find it quite simple to structure the session around the questions.

How Do You Get Going?

The leader should encourage prospective participants to consider the cost carefully. An effective, life-changing experience will take some time, effort...and money. Are group members willing to invest time for the study and money for the book? Once participants are committed, it is probably best for the group leader to have the materials available for them at the first meeting.

The leader should explain purposes and procedures at the first meeting. A quick overview of the book and study guide would be helpful. Explain the weekly assignments and the necessity of completing them *before* each study session.

Enthusiasm is contagious. What could be more exciting than learning to become a redemptive person, one who attracts people to the Savior? The leader should cultivate his own enthusiasm for this study. If the leader is enthused, the group will soon be infected with enthusiasm too.

SESSION 1

The Enterprise Called Evangelism
Introduction

Purposes

- To study Christ's plan for worldwide evangelism.
- To consider some reasons why his plan has not been implemented.
- To examine some of the caricatures of evangelism which hinder the successful realization of Christ's plan.

Scriptural Input

Read Matthew 28:16-20. In this passage on the Great Commission, Jesus instructed his disciples to gather at a particular mountain in Galilee. How did they respond when Christ joined them at that mountain retreat (v. 17)?

Some doubted (v. 17). Christ obviously anticipated these doubts. His statement (vv. 18-20) is designed to answer their doubts. Study carefully his response to their worship and doubt. Based on Christ's response, what concerns caused the disciples apprehension and doubt?

Read Acts 1:8. This is a foundational text on evangelism, focusing on divine strength and divine strategy. In what specific ways does God's Spirit empower Christians for effective witness? Acts 1:8 is also a lesson in geography: Jerusalem, Judea, Samaria, and the ends of the earth. Acts 2 records that the church was born in Jerusalem. History records its extension into Judea, Samaria, and the ends of the earth. Is the order significant? If so, describe your personal Jerusalem. Your church's Jerusalem.

Thought Questions

1. Write down the first word that comes to your mind when you hear the words "Great Commission." Share it with the group.

2. What evangelism models (pp. 17-19) have you been involved with?

3. What doubts haunt you concerning your personal part in fulfilling the Great Commission?

4. Arnold Toynbee said that "most people have not rejected Christianity but a caricature." Do you agree? Describe some of the caricatures non-Christians have about Christianity.

Action Steps

1. List the names of several pre-Christians in your Jerusalem.

2. Use this list as a daily prayer sheet. Commit yourself to pray for each person daily during the duration of this study.

3. Ready to risk? How about inviting a pre-Christian over for dinner or dessert or just for coffee? If nothing else, make an effort to be friendly in a specific, concrete way.

SESSION 2

Embarking on a Pilgrimage to Beauty
Chapter 1

Purposes

- To consider the role of beauty in God's evangelism strategy.
- To examine the bride motif as a pattern for evangelism.
- To define evangelism in the light of Christ's bride, the church.
- To consider Christ's communication strategy as a model to follow.

Scriptural Input

Read Ezekiel 16:1-14, which describes Israel's pilgrimage from the rubbish heap to royalty. As God's bride, Israel's beauty spread throughout the nations (16:14). What was the source of her beauty? What did the nations see when Israel's beauty was on display? List specific ways God's beauty was revealed through Israel.

Read Ephesians 5:22-33. What does comparing the church to a bride have to do with evangelism? Is the bride's attractiveness more verbal or nonverbal?

Read John 1:14-18. Christ became human to reveal the Father and redeem man. His revelatory mission spanned thirty-three years, his redemptive mission a few days. He declared that "if you've seen me, you've seen the Father." Christ's actions and words have revealed the Father's love, holiness, justice, compassion, and mercy. List specific examples.

Read Matthew 13:1-8, 24-30. Your mission is to make visible the invisible God, following the pattern of Christ in the first incarnation. The Bible calls you a living epistle, a shining star, a fragrant aroma, a wise fisherman, a beautiful bride, salt and light, and good (beautiful) seed. What do these descriptions imply about the ways we communicate the gospel?

The first parable in Matthew 13 focuses on the quality of the soil. The second highlights the quality of the seed. Why is it important to be sensitive to *both* conditions? What happens when we are inconsiderate of the condition of the soil? The seed? In the natural realm, cultivation precedes sowing and reaping. Is this true in the spiritual realm?

Thought Questions

1. How then, can shallow, hard, weed-filled souls be cultivated in preparation for seed planting?

2. Cultivation (an appeal to the *heart* through the building of a relationship) is stage one of the evangelism process. List specific things Christians can do to cultivate a soul.

3. Sowing (an appeal to the *mind* through the communication of revelation) is stage two of the evangelism process. List specific ways in which seeds can be planted.

4. Reaping (an appeal to the *will* in anticipation of a response) is stage three of the evangelism process. Is every Christian expected to be a reaper?

5. The Mormons have developed a program for expansion which involves monitoring local maternity wards. Upon the birth of a child, a Mormon visits the new mother and offers to provide meals for a week when she returns home. Is this a good strategy? Is its primary appeal the heart, the mind, or the will? What do you predict its success will be? Why?

Action Steps

1. List specific strategies for cultivation which would be workable for you in your neighborhood.

2. Continue praying for your list of pre-Christians.

3. Get out your calendar and set aside an evening for some type of cultivation activity.

4. Call a pre-Christian friend and get something scheduled.

SESSION 3

Avoiding Evil Instead of Its Appearance
Chapter 2

Purposes

- To consider the role of culture in determining church form and structure.

- To survey the four positions Christians assume when a debatable issue arises.

- To weigh the possibility of avoiding the appearance of evil while being salt and light.

- To consider guidelines for relating to the non-Christian world.

Scriptural Input

Read the foreword to *Life-Style Evangelism.* On the basis of Matthew 10:24-25, Luke 7:33-34, and Luke 15:1-2, do you believe Haddon Robinson's comments are correct?

Read Galatians 2:3-5,11-14. Paul rebuked Peter because Peter ate with Gentiles when Jews were not present, but refused to eat with them when the Jews were present. Peter did not wish to offend the Jews. What was the real issue? Did Paul's command force Peter to appear evil to Jewish believers?

Read Romans 14. Does the man whose faith allows him to eat everything (v. 2) eat without sinning? Does God accept him (v. 3)?

If a weak brother violates his conscience by eating meat offered to idols, does he sin? Can two Christians, then, do the identical thing and one sin and the other not sin?

List the responsibilities of the stronger brother (14:1,3,10,13, 15,19-23). List the responsibilities of the weaker brother (14:3,10, 13,19).

Thought Questions

1. How do culturally-imposed barriers hinder evangelism? Cite some examples.

2. Using the list on pages 40-41, decide which of the statements are biblical and which are cultural. Compare your answers with the rest of the group.

3. Select a nonmoral, neutral action or behavior you are not free to participate in. In relationship to this issue, are you: 1) a professional weaker brother; 2) a susceptible weaker brother; or 3) a nonparticipating mature brother?

4. How might a professional weaker brother hinder the evangelistic efforts of a local church? How might a participating mature brother, by his abuse of liberty, hinder the evangelistic efforts of a local church?

5. Compromise is a red-flag word. What does it mean? When is it legitimate and necessary? When is it not an option?

Action Steps

1. Meditate a bit on the flavor of your life. Have you been a professional weaker brother? Have you abused liberty? Who have you offended by your misuse of liberty or by your judgmental attitude?

2. Write a descriptive paragraph about yourself from the viewpoint of a non-Christian neighbor or work associate. What attitudes, cultural distinctives, or limitations do you have which may be hindrances to reaching non-Christians?

3. In what ways, if any, are you hindered in your evangelism efforts by the attitudes and expectations of your local church?

4. Keep on cultivating and praying! Affirm a pre-Christian friend by giving him a friendship card. Invite someone to join you at a coffee break. Comment about some of their positive qualities.

Eating Meat and Evangelizing
Chapter 3

Purposes

- To consider a Christian response to culture.
- To affirm the necessity of maintaining a radical difference.
- To delineate the Christian responsibility to be a redemptive neighbor.

Scriptural Input

Read Matthew 5:1-16. The eight beatitudes describe a wholesome, balanced, God-flavored person. The kind God wants to deploy into the world. The first four qualities focus Godward, the second four manward. Note that the first quality in the first series of four (poor in spirit) is the basis of the first quality in the second series of four (merciful). Following the same pattern, do you see similar cause-and-effect relationships between the remaining qualities?

Put together a written profile of a God-flavored person using the qualities described in Matthew 5:1-16 as a starting point.

What dimensions of Christian witness are illustrated by the figure of salt? Light?

When salt loses its saltiness, there is a change in its character. When light is hidden, the problem is concealment, not loss of character. How do Christians lose their flavor? How do they lose their visibility?

What is the result when non-Christians see and experience the good deeds of caring Christians (v. 16b)? Why is this so?

Read 1 Corinthians 9:19-23. Why does Paul make such a big point of "becoming"? What are the implications for evangelism?

Read Luke 7:33-34. Compare and contrast the ministries of John the Baptist and Jesus Christ. How were they the same? How were they different?

Thought Questions

1. What factors can help a Christian maintain the critical balance between radical difference and radical identification?

2. How do you accept a person without condoning his lifestyle?

3. What are some rights a caring Christian might have to set aside if he is to reach his non-Christian friend?

4. What are some of the yellow lights that flash when you are around non-Christians?

5. Do you tend to follow the model of John the Baptist or Jesus Christ in your personal evangelism efforts? Do you readily affirm and support those who gravitate to the other model?

Action Steps

1. List some necessary steps or disciplines you need to initiate or reactivate in order to deepen your commitment to a radical difference.

2. What simple, practical steps can you take this week toward radical identification?

3. Is this the week you make your home circle an open circle as another step toward being a redemptive neighbor?

4. As you continue to pray specifically for lost friends, God will open doors for you to serve. Look for them this week. Don't miss them. Remember, it also is important to let them serve you!

5. Think for a moment about some of your neighbors. What are some ways you can apply 1 Corinthians 9:22b in your relationship with them (see pp. 65-72)?

Practicing the Presence in Evangelism
Chapter 4

Purposes

- To explore evangelism as a process.
- To compare and contrast various categories of evangelism.
- To consider human need as a starting point for evangelism.

Scriptural Input

Evangelism as a process moves through at least three phases. First, cultivating (or presence), which is an appeal to the heart through the building of a *relationship.* Second, sowing (or proclamation), which is an appeal to the mind through the communication of *revelation.* Third, reaping (or persuasion), which is an appeal to the *will* looking for a response.

Study carefully John 4:1-26. Our Lord's encounter with the immoral Samaritan woman illustrates in abbreviated form the process of evangelism. In what ways did he cultivate? Sow? Reap? How did he appeal to her heart, her mind, and her will?

We've seen that the Christian is to be God-flavored; he is to be displaying the universals of God's character through the particulars of everyday living. Second Corinthians 3:1-3 describes the Christian as a living epistle. Who is the author? What is the message written upon? Who reads the epistle?

In Galatians 5:19-23, some X-rated, flesh-produced "reading materials" are contrasted with the fruits of the Spirit of God. Name the God-flavored fruits and write a one-sentence description for each. When the Spirit is the author, what do living epistle readers read?

Read Matthew 5:16; Ephesians 2:8-10; Titus 3:8; 1 Peter 2:11-17; 3:15; 4:7-11, 19. The theme of good works runs through all these verses. List some specific results that take place when non-Christians observe and participate in our good works. Notice that God has made plans for our involvement in acts of service that will reveal to others the universals of his character.

The Book of Acts emphasizes proclamational evangelism (*read* Acts 2:14; 4:1-2; 5:42; 17:16-17; 18:24-28). The epistles emphasize relational evangelism (*read* 1 Corinthians 10:31-33; 2 Corinthians 3:2; Colossians 4:5-6; 1 Peter 2:12-17; 3:1-2). As the local church matures and becomes established in a community, what happens in its approach to evangelism?

Thought Questions

1. What are some of the advantages of proclamational evangelism? What kinds of skills are necessary to be effective in proclamation?

2. What are some of the disadvantages of confrontational/intrusional evangelism? What kinds of skills are necessary for this approach?

3. A child's mind swings open easily, like a screen door. An adult mind is like a bank vault door…it resists opening and swings slowly. Discuss some of the key factors involved in getting vault doors open (see pp. 82-91). What did God use in your life to open the door?

4. Explain in your own words the meaning of the phrase "when love is felt, the message is heard."

5. What are some needs you have identified in your non-Christian neighbors or business associates? What social, emotional, mental, spiritual, and physical needs have you observed? How can the gospel meet those needs?

Action Steps

1. Prayer is not part of the ministry, it *is* the ministry. Don't let up on your regular, systematic prayer for your non-Christian friends.

2. List some hobbies, interests, relationships, or skills you share in common with some of your non-Christian friends.

3. Begin plans for a block party, an open house, a seasonal party, or an informal dessert.

4. Begin familiarizing yourself with good literature (books, tracts, pamphlets) which might be helpful in the seed-planting (proclamational) stage. Topics related to marriage, home, family, prophecy, and Israel are often well received. Buy some to have on hand for that opportune moment.

S E S S I O N   6

Evangelism and the Church Member
Chapter 5

Purposes

- To demonstrate the role of edification in evangelism.
- To consider the qualities of the person the church wants to deploy into the world.
- To study a verbal portrait of a dynamic New Testament church.

Scriptural Input

Our Lord was the master teacher. His goal was to see truth become operational in life. His mission was not to fill jugs but to light lamps. According to Luke 6:40, what is the evidence that a pupil has been fully taught?

Values are caught, not taught. Faith is caught, not taught. We copy those we care for. How is this truth illustrated in 1 Thessalonians 1:4-7? Paul did not say, "You know how we lectured among you." He said, "You know how we *lived.*" The personal pronoun "you" occurs with a verb four times in verses 5b-7. List the verbs. Note the progressive transfer of values.

Read Ephesians 4:11-16, which describes the role of the church in shaping and influencing the life of the believer. Gifted men and women are God's instruments to shape and mold the lives of others. What is the ultimate evidence of the church's effectiveness as a transforming community (v. 16)? Note that its effectiveness is dependent upon the proper working of *each* individual *part.*

Read Acts 2:42-47, a case study of an early New Testament church. Using the text as a basis for investigation, write a profile of a member of this early church. Answer such questions as, What did he do? How did he relate to God? To fellow Christians? To the world? Was he positive or negative? What was his reputation? What influences shaped his life? How did God respond to such people?

Thought Questions

1. In many respects a Christian matures in the same way a Japanese child becomes Japanese. It's a process of socialization. The child attends no classes, listens to no lectures, takes no pills. He catches Japanese from the Japanese! He becomes like his teacher. Likewise, the Christian must become good news before he shares good news. Using the socialization model, how does the body of Christ (the church) influence and shape the individual believer?

2. What are some evidences that edification is beginning to take place in the believer's life? Why is edification the key to evangelism?

3. Describe the role of fellowship in the growth process of the believer. What are three major hindrances to the healthy fellowship of believers?

4. Notice the list of "one anothers" on pages 102-3. What relationship do these qualities have to the evangelism effectiveness of the local church?

Discuss some of the cause-and-effect relationships between teaching, fellowship, and worship. What are some differences between genuine worship and many of our worship services? What is the role of worship in motivation for service?

Action Steps

1. Continue regular prayer for specific pre-Christian friends.

2. Evaluate your own fellowship, worship, and service experiences. Do you have significant fellowship experiences with Christians? Does your experience of worship serve as a catalyst for service? What can you do to create more significant worship experiences?

3. Continue reaching out toward your non-Christian friends. Be creative!

SESSION 7

Evangelism and the Church Body
Chapter 6

Purposes

- To consider the marks of a healthy church.

- To examine four negative qualities which damage the redemptive mission of the church.

- To discuss four divine signposts which are prerequisites for effective evangelism.

- To reinforce the role of authenticity in Christian life and witness.

Scriptural Input

Read Acts 2:42-47. These courageous Christians were products of their corporate community, and as they deployed themselves into the world God added daily to their number. List the four qualities of a church which deploys healthy, serving people.

In Matthew 16:1-12, Jesus is instructing the future founders of his church. He warns them to avoid the leaven of the Pharisees and Sadducees. What did he mean? What danger does this leaven pose for the church?

First Corinthians 5:1-13 describes the leaven of impurity. What is its impact upon the redemptive mission of the church? How did the Corinthian church misinterpret Paul's instructions (vv. 9-11)?

Galatians 5:1-13 describes the leaven of legalism. In what ways does it hinder the redemptive mission of the church?

John 13:34-35 gives the non-Christian the right to judge the reality of the Christian's profession of faith. What is the determining evidence? What does it prove to the non-Christian?

John 17:23 suggests that unity has evangelistic impact. What is the difference between Christian unity and uniformity?

First Peter 2:12 discusses the power of good works. What role do they have in evangelism?

Hope is another divine signpost (1 Peter 3:15). Describe an imaginary situation in which a nonbeliever observes and is influenced by a believer's hope. What conditions are necessary for hope to be seen?

Thought Questions

1. How does accountability contribute to the fellowship and health of the church? Are men or women more apt to be open to accountability? What barriers hinder accountability?

2. Why might a pastor feel threatened by accountability? How can a pastor be encouraged to be open to accountability?

3. Worship is a barometer of spiritual health and vitality. What is the relationship between worship and witness (pp. 113-14)?

4. Discuss the relationship between edification and evangelism. Which should be the focus of the Sunday morning service? Why?

5. Why would Christ allow his disciples to offend the Pharisees?

6. Define authenticity (p. 118). Why is this a difficult quality to attain?

7. Is optimism a biblical necessity (p. 128)? Describe its impact.

Action Steps

1. Do a fellowship analysis. Do you have close friends who hold you accountable?

2. Analyze your worship. What steps can you take to enhance your corporate and private communion with God?

3. What specific good works are you involved in with your neighbors? What needs do they have that you can meet? What needs can they meet in your life?

4. Keep looking for opportunities to serve.

SESSION 8

Evangelism and the Church Leadership
Chapter 7

Purposes

- To consider the role model of the church leader.

- To explore leadership qualities.

- To examine the impact of a healthy leadership team on the corporate church fellowship.

Scriptural Input

Read 1 Peter 5:1-4. Church leaders are called shepherds. List the qualities that come to mind when you think about a shepherd.

From the descriptions used in 1 Peter 5:1-3, write a job description of a church leader. Note such items as attitudes, motives, relational qualities, and responsibilities.

The elder is never to "lord it over the flock." What does this mean? How can one lead without lording (v. 3b)? What role does the leader's example play in the educational mission of the church?

Read 1 Peter 5:5-6. To what kind of people does God give special grace (attention or enablement)? What kind of people does God single out for increased visibility and effectiveness? Note that Peter's command to "clothe yourselves with humility" includes the elders.

Do you know anyone who demonstrates humility? What are some qualities that characterize that person's life?

Read 1 Timothy 3:1-13. Write your own definition for at least six of these qualities required of leaders.

Paul declares that candidates for leadership must demonstrate their capability to create and sustain a healthy, vibrant home where beauty dwells (vv. 4-5). Why does God insist on an exemplary home life?

The leader's home circle is to be an open one. He is required to be hospitable (v. 2). Why? Discuss the power of hospitality (Hebrews 13:2; Romans 12:13).

Thought Questions

1. The relationships between board members are crucial. Describe the board relationships in your church. How have these board members influenced the attitudes and productivity of your church?

2. Is unanimity in decision making a realistic way for boards to function? What are advantages and disadvantages of such a policy?

3. The leader must be able to teach. What is the difference between teaching with authority and teaching in an authoritarian manner?

Action Steps

1. Put your church leaders on your daily prayer list. They are special targets of satanic opposition.

2. Avoid all public criticism of your leaders. If you have criticism, share it only with the appropriate person.

3. Help educate your elders. Take the initiative to purchase and provide them with books that will help them develop biblical philosophies of evangelism and discipleship.

4. Encourage leaders to attend leadership training conferences.

5. If you are a church leader, guard the unity; resist critical people; be a peacemaker.

6. Continue to pray for your pre-Christian friends.

SESSION 9

Evangelism and the Pastor
Chapter 8

Purposes

- To consider the biblical qualities of a mature pastor.

- To understand the pressures unique to the pastorate.

- To consider the determinative role of the pastor in shaping the attitudes and actions of the leadership team.

- To explore opportunities for you to encourage and strengthen your pastor.

Scriptural Input

Review 1 Timothy 3:1-7; Titus 1:5-9; 1 Peter 5:1-4. What special temptations and dangers must the pastor be alert to?

Read Philippians 3:7-11. Paul spells out the central desires of his life (v. 10). List them. What was he willing to give in exchange for these goals (vv. 7-8)? How do you think Paul's goals would have influenced your life if you had been his friend?

Read Hebrews 11:1-16. What delights the Father's heart (v. 6)? Compare the impact of a pastor who is a man of faith with one who lacks it.

What is the significance of the statement "they admitted that they were aliens and strangers on earth"? How would this attitude influence the life and ministry of a pastor and his flock? If this world is not our home, why are we here?

Read 2 Corinthians 3:12-18. Why is it unnecessary for Christians today to veil their faces? How do openness and authenticity strengthen the impact of a pastor's life and ministry? Why are pastors especially prone to be inauthentic?

Thought Questions

1. Go through the checklist on page 145. Compare your answers with a friend or fellow study group member. How do

your expectations affect the pastor? Give both positive and negative influences.

2. How do the personality and beliefs of the pastor influence his leadership team? Be specific.

3. Galatians 6:1 says that when a brother is overtaken in a fault, spiritually mature believers should seek to restore him. Does the principle apply to pastors? Should the pastor be accountable to a group of his peers? Why or why not?

4. What special dynamics or situations exist in a pastoral ministry which might encourage moral failure? How can a local church help a pastor in this area?

5. Most pastors have not been effective in reaching their neighbors. Why is this true? How does this affect the evangelism ministry of the church?

Action Steps

1. List changes you believe need to be made to strengthen your pastor as a role model. Turn this list into a prayer list and intercede faithfully on his behalf.

2. List some specific things you can do to encourage and strengthen your pastor's effectiveness.

3. Christ wants to use your legs, arms, mouth, and heart today and all this week. Pray for specific, definite opportunities for him to love the lost through you.

4. Perhaps you can use this week to take Christ into your neighbor's home and life. List some specific, simple ways in which he might desire to use you this week.

5. Continue to pray for boldness and open doors.

Your Home and Evangelistic Bible Studies
Chapter 9

Purposes

- To study biblical models of hospitality.
- To consider the home as a center for evangelism.
- To understand the unique dynamics and necessary ingredients of an evangelistic Bible study.
- To consider the crucial role of the host and hostess in a evangelistic study.

Scriptural Input

Read 1 Timothy 3:1-7 and 1 Peter 4:9. The average Christian expects the church to instruct us in how to worship and the world to teach us how to celebrate. We have neglected the important dimensions of joyous celebration of special occasions, events, and milestones in life. What does it mean to offer hospitality to one another?

A hospitable person is one who loves strangers. *Read* Leviticus 19:18, 33-34, and Deuteronomy 10:18-19. Who is the model of hospitality?

Much of Jesus' ministry centered around the home and hospitality, and demonstrates that hospitality enhances the communication of the gospel. *Read* Mark 1:29-31; 2:1-12; Luke 10:30-42. List the actions and attitudes of a hospitable person.

In Acts 16:22-34, Paul makes the interesting statement that if the Philippian jailer believes, both he and his house will be saved. What events happened from the time Paul and Silas entered the jailer's home until they left? What did his wife and children see, hear, and participate in? What contribution did this experience make toward the salvation of the entire family?

Thought Questions

1. Why did discussion stop when my friend suggested that the folks at the bar talk about Jesus Christ (p. 163)?

2. In what ways can embarrassment be a barrier to hospitality? What other barriers to hospitality can you identify?

3 . How has the doctrine of separation influenced our views of hospitality?

4. What are some significant differences between a regular home Bible study and an evangelistic home Bible study (pp. 164-65)? Why must these differences be maintained?

5. Describe the kind of atmosphere in which the non-Christian is most likely to be comfortable and ready to become involved with biblical truth (pp. 165-69).

6 . What contribution do food and other refreshments make to the impact of redemptive hospitality?

Action Steps

1. Consider the possibility of starting a home Bible study. List possible participants. Determine the most effective host and hostess.

2. Who is best equipped to lead the discussion? What topic would be best for your group of friends?

3. What other Christians could join with you in this outreach effort?

4. What materials can you locate as possible subject matter? (I recommend the evangelistic Bible study developed by Search Ministries, *Who Is This Man Jesus?* This is available at most Christian bookstores or by writing Multnomah Books, Questar Publishers, Inc., P. O. Box 1720, Sisters, OR 97759.)

5. Continue praying . . . specifically and daily.

SESSION 11

Your Nonbelieving Neighbor
Chapter 10

Purposes

- To visualize specific steps for reaching your neighborhood.

- To consider contact points you can utilize in your neighborhood.

- To see holidays as significant times for building relationships.

- To learn how to be a seed-planter.

Scriptural Input

Read John 4:1-38. What barriers did Jesus overcome by relating to this Samaritan woman of ill repute? Why were the disciples surprised (v. 27)?

In John 4:34-38 Jesus likens evangelism to sowing and reaping. Describe reaping. How is it different from sowing and cultivating? What kinds of things did those "others" do? In what ways is the labor of those others "hard work" (v. 38)?

Thought Questions

1. What is the role of vision in success of any kind? How does vision influence evangelism? What do you visualize as your part in reaching your neighborhood?

2. How do you locate the "schooling fish" (pp. 175-76) in your neighborhood? People will not receive Christ through you if they will not receive you first. What steps are you taking to build relationships with your neighbors?

3. Why would a real estate firm adopt a sales strategy as described on page 177? What principles of influence are illustrated by this model?

4. Brainstorm possible topics of conversation between Christians and non-Christians.

5. Describe an evening social event that would be enjoyable for a non-Christian. What factors need to be present? What should be avoided?

Action Steps

1. List contact points you have with some of your non-Christian friends (see pp. 180-81 for suggestions).

2. Begin planning for a holiday event you can use as an opportunity for hospitality. Get it on your calendar!

3. List ways you are able to be of service to your neighbors. What vocational skills do you have that you can use to meet some of the needs of your non-Christian friends?

4. Preview and buy some Christian literature to give to a non-Christian friend.

5. Begin working with your church leadership to plan some evangelistic harvest vehicles (pp. 184-86).

6. Memorize the four steps in "seed planting" (pp. 186-89).

7. Pray for opportunities to plant seeds with your pre-Christian friends...and start planting!

S E S S I O N   1 2

Your Personal Message of Evangelism
Chapter 11

Purposes

- To learn how to share the words of the gospel.
- To understand signs of spiritual readiness.
- To develop a logical approach to leading people to Christ.
- To distinguish between good and bad methods of sharing Christ.

Scriptural Input

Read Matthew 28:16-20 and Acts 1:8. What is the mandate from the Master? What help is promised? What is the practical significance of "Jerusalem, Judea, and Samaria, and the ends of the earth"?

Read Acts 17:16-21. Note that verse 17 says Paul reasoned with his audience. What implications does this have for evangelistic methodology?

Read Acts 18:4-5. What key verbs indicate Paul's approach to proclaiming the gospel? What was the heart of his message?

Read John 1:12; 3:16,36; Acts 4:12; Romans 3:23; 6:23; 1 Corinthians 15:3-4; Ephesians 2:1-10; Titus 3:5. What is the gospel? What basic truths need to be communicated if the non-Christian is truly going to "hear the words"?

Thought Questions

1. Paul prayed for open doors. It's foolish to go through a closed one. What are some signs that doors are opening in the life of a non-Christian friend (p. 192)?

2. What is the difference between asking a person if he is a Christian and asking him where he is on his spiritual pilgrimage?

3. In the *opportunity statement* (p. 194) why is "sometime" included? What difference could it make?

4. What would you do if you asked your friend the *interest question* (p. 195) and he said "no"?

5. How does knowing ahead of time the three *decision questions* (p. 196) help your gospel presentation?

6. Everyone uses a method. "No method" is a method. What are some of the characteristics of a good method (pp. 198-99)?

7. What is the role of attitudes in effective communication? How does it influence the content?

8. What is the advantage of writing out a presentation? How should you handle questions that are raised during your presentation?

Action Steps

1. Memorize ten key verses you can use when presenting the gospel.

2. Choose an effective evangelism method and practice presenting it to a member of your study group or another Christian friend. (The Navigators' *Bridge to Life* and Campus Crusade for Christ's *Four Spiritual Laws* are two suggestions.)

3. Memorize the three *decision questions.*

4. Pray for boldness and for opportunities to explain the gospel to your pre-Christian friends.

Scripture Index

1 Peter

2 Peter

1 John

2 John

Have you read the other books in our Classical Critical Concern series?

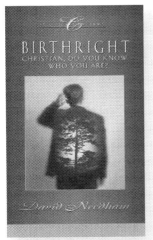

David Needham asks "Christian, do you know who you are?" in this remarkable and easy-to-understand rere-lease of his book about the Christian's birthright. He offers fresh insight into the theological problem of Christian identity, biblically based teaching, and a challenge for personal enrichment and further Bible study. *Birthright* achieves an excellent balance between the theological and the practical. The author's sincerity and candid writing style are guaranteed to buoy the spirits of readers.

ISBN 1-59052-666-X

Does God have a perfect will for each Christian? Does it matter? Can you be absolutely sure of God's individual will for your life? In an easy-to-follow narrative style, Garry Friesen examines the prevalent views on God's will today, then rejects them to propose a different view that he believes more accurately reflects biblical teaching. This rerelease of *Decision Making* takes up the practical issues of choosing a mate, picking a career, giving of one's resources, and areas of disagreement between Christians to give readers a new approach to knowing the will of God.

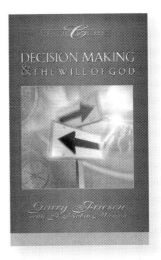

ISBN 1-57673-321-1

Printed in the United States
by Baker & Taylor Publisher Services